DISCLAIMER

The author and publisher are providing this book and its contents on an "as is" basis and make no representations or warranties of any kind with respect to this book or its contents. The author and publisher disclaim all such representations and warranties, including but not limited to warranties of merchantability. In addition, the author and publisher do not represent or warrant that the information accessible via this book is accurate, complete, or current.

Except as specifically stated in this book, neither the author nor publisher, nor any authors, contributors, or other representatives will be liable for damages arising out of or in connection with the use of this book. This is a comprehensive limitation of liability that applies to all damages of any kind, including (without limitation) compensatory; direct, indirect, or consequential damages; loss of data, income, or profit; loss of or damage to property; and claims of third parties.

This Book Comes With Free Bonus Puzzles
Available Here:

BestActivityBooks.com/WSBONUS20

5 TIPS TO START!

1) HOW TO SOLVE

The Puzzles are in a Classic Format:

- Words are hidden without breaks (no spaces, dashes, ...)
- Orientation: Forward & Backward, Up & Down or
  in Diagonal (can be in both directions)
- Words can overlap or cross each other

2) ACTIVE LEARNING

To encourage learning actively, a space is provided next to each word to write down the translation. The **DICTIONARY** allows you to verify and expand your knowledge. You can look up and write down each translation, find the words in the Puzzle then add them to your vocabulary!

3) TAG YOUR WORDS

Have you tried using a tag system? For example, you could mark the words which have been difficult to find with a cross, the ones you loved with a star, new words with a triangle, rare words with a diamond and so on...

4) ORGANIZE YOUR LEARNING

We also offer a convenient **NOTEBOOK** at the end of this edition.
Whether on vacation, travelling or at home, you can easily organize your new knowledge without needing a second notebook!

5) FINISHED?

Go to the bonus section: **MONSTER CHALLENGE** to find a free game offered at the end of this edition!

Want more fun and learning activities? It's **Fast and Simple!**
An entire Game Book Collection just **one click away!**

Find your next challenge at:

BestActivityBooks.com/MyNextWordSearch

Ready, Set... Go!

Did you know there are around 7,000 different languages in the world? Words are precious.

We love languages and have been working hard to make the highest quality books for you. Our ingredients?

A selection of indispensable learning themes, three big slices of fun, then we add a spoonful of difficult words and a pinch of rare ones. We serve them up with care and a maximum of delight so you can solve the best word games and have fun learning!

Your feedback is essential. You can be an active participant in the success of this book by leaving us a review. Tell us what you liked most in this edition!

Here is a short link which will take you to your order page.

BestBooksActivity.com/Review50

Thanks for your help and enjoy the Game!

Linguas Classics Team

1 - Antiques

```
Ö  E  Z  C  W  L  S  L  V  B  O  K  E  V
F  Ý  I  B  O  M  Q  O  P  A  W  Ö  W  F
M  T  G  E  Z  E  B  V  V  H  A  N  E  O
U  E  N  O  I  S  K  U  A  A  D  E  W  M
Ý  Ý  K  L  Ş  C  P  M  H  U  A  Z  R  E
O  I  H  D  D  L  R  Z  Z  A  N  T  E  R
G  S  I  R  E  L  A  G  I  H  K  N  Ý  K
A  Ä  G  A  O  P  U  R  L  G  W  Y  I  E
Ý  H  H  L  E  D  S  P  Y  G  J  A  K  Z
A  U  O  R  B  A  D  A  T  Y  D  Ä  L  Y
M  O  L  A  D  I  K  E  L  D  I  Ş  S  B
T  G  L  R  E  L  E  Ň  Ň  E  T  A  R  T
O  K  T  A  M  M  Y  G  D  N  T  L  B  F
R  E  L  K  I  L  Ş  I  U  P  O  K  J  Z
```

ART	MAÝA GOÝUM
AUKSION	EWEWREÝ
HAKYKY	KÖNE
MERKEZ	BAHA
TEŇŇELER	HÄSIÝET
KARARLAR	DIKELDIŞ
BEZEG	MEKDEP
OWADAN	IŞLIKLER
ÖÝ GOŞLARY	ADATY DÄL
GALERI	GYMMAT

2 - Food #1

```
T G H P J D Q J A P T U N A
Ý Ü P E K I U L R A S G M G
Ü S R N I N Z Z P N H I E Z
S A Z Ä L N O M A N N I S K
I L A D R S A M A N Ç Y C Ö
H L E R A P Ç N X Z T L Y P
A A Q Ü G Y A O D X H E V E
R N P D F H B M R M J N U Ň
A D N J E O G I O B B V C A
H Y D D V F S L K R A H J K
Ş Ş E K E R K A R O T S Y G
E I T U R N I P A T D P Y E
C X R A P R I K O T R J B O
U H H E E N B A S I L V N J
```

APRIKOT	ARAHIS
ARPA	DÜRDÄNE
BASIL	SALLANDY
KAROT	DUZ
SINNAMON	ÇORBASY
GARLIK	ÝÜPEKI
ŞIRE	SAMANÇY
LIMON	ŞEKER
SÜÝT	TUNA
KÖPEŇ	TURNIP

3 - Measurements

```
W  L  I  T  R  K  K  O  N  L  I  K  M  R
B  O  Ý  I  F  S  I  L  O  U  Z  U  E  G
M  V  U  O  M  X  L  L  T  Y  T  L  R  F
L  X  Z  L  C  C  Ň  N  O  A  A  Ň  K  Y
T  H  Y  U  V  J  I  S  T  G  M  U  E  A
K  Q  N  P  E  T  G  G  Q  F  R  Ç  Z  E
S  C  L  J  Q  Ý  A  R  P  G  O  A  Z  J
M  K  Y  L  M  A  D  A  N  O  F  S  M  R
A  A  K  W  A  B  K  M  R  J  T  H  C  B
N  K  S  H  R  G  E  R  E  K  I  J  D  F
I  N  Ç  S  G  D  U  Y  P  O  N  G  F  M
F  Z  I  E  A  N  Q  R  R  C  U  V  P  O
N  J  I  I  A  L  M  I  N  U  D  A  V  K
H  T  X  R  E  L  Y  S  Ö  U  M  G  I  K
```

BAÝT
MERKEZ
ONLIK
GEREK
ÇUŇLUK
GRAM
BOÝ
INÇ
KILOGRAM
UNIT-FORMAT

UZYNLYK
LITR
MASSALY
MINUDA
ONADAMLYK
TON
SÖUMGI
AGRAM
GIŇLIK

4 - Farm #2

```
B U G D A Ý V B J Q F K Y B
T R A K T O R E M R E F A E
S Ý M I W E Z T Z B A U F Ý
U H Ü H I V L J T Ä C R R I
W A W S H G G V I Ş M X P W
A Ý F A R U A O M G G H Z A
R W T W R Z F B Ý Ä U Q T T
Y A S U Q Y Q V I U F S K G
Ş N R A B L L I M D N I W E
L L I L U A Y O R Ç A R D W
L A T L I X K N Q R R Q R L
A R P A M G O M E Ý A D O W
M F G O A W R C P L Q U Q F
A M H Y V T N U Ö R D E K L
```

HAÝWANLAR	GUZY
ARPA	LLAMA
BARN	MEÝADOW
BEÝIW	SÜÝT
KORN	ORÇARD
ÖRDEK	GOÝUN
FERMER	TRAKTOR
IÝMIT	BÄŞGÄ
MIWE	BUGDAÝ
SUWARYŞ	WINDMILL

5 - Books

```
W B P U E L F T W M K N G T
S Q I X N D K A A E O Z Ö E
S K F D F A E Y S R H I R R
K O L H O Z Ý B I M Y P N J
E E A H I L K B I E R H Ü I
T P D E K K L Q A R P I Ş M
N I V K I K L Y G Ş O G R E
O K E A L P O E M A Y M O S
K U N Ý I I S G Ü L K I K A
A K T A K Ç E P E R I V Y H
O O U A J O I I W O F R J Y
U F R D Q C R P G T C C Y P
J R E M Q G E Y I W J S B A
T R A G I K S J S A K F Q H
```

ADVENTURE
AWTOR
KOLHOZ
KONTEKS
IKILIK
EPIK
TARYH
GÜLKI
TERJIME
EDEBI

NAÝBAŞY
ÇEPER
SAHYPA
POEMA
GOŞGY
OKYJY
GÖRNÜŞ
SERIES
HEKAÝA
TRAGIK

6 - Meditation

```
D  X  K  M  D  Y  M  M  A  K  Z  H  C  Z
Z  U  X  Ö  Ä  D  Z  A  I  C  N  A  Ý  O
S  F  Ý  T  Ň  H  P  Y  L  H  K  B  Q  I
W  Z  Y  G  C  L  I  Ş  K  T  E  I  D  S
A  C  A  A  U  G  I  R  Y  A  M  T  M  D
Y  G  A  B  N  L  W  A  L  G  T  L  N  N
P  I  K  I  R  Y  A  G  T  I  E  E  T  W
L  L  B  O  D  K  Y  R  A  B  L  R  F  L
K  M  Ş  Y  L  A  Ç  G  H  E  U  I  C  J
D  M  U  S  I  K  V  Z  A  T  B  I  K  W
P  I  K  I  R  L  E  R  R  A  A  G  M  S
G  Ö  R  N  Ü  Ş  W  G  A  R  K  M  T  B
S  N  T  T  W  E  Y  M  P  U  U  Y  V  P
I  E  H  V  I  E  T  E  Y  S  H  A  Ş  C
```

KABUL ETMEK	KÖŇLI
OÝAN	MUSIK
ÇALYŞ	TEBIGAT
GARŞY	GÖRNÜŞ
DUÝGULAR	PARAHATLYK
HABITLER	ŞAHSY .ET
BAGT	SURAT
MÄHIRLILIK	DYMMAK
AKYL	PIKIRLER
PIKIR	

7 - Days and Months

```
E P Y X E Ý M A Y I N J M B
B R A D N E L A K B O U A D
N R Y O D K H L R I Ý M G U
E Z G Z W Ş I E A T A A T Ş
Ş E N B E E X Ý P Z B G Y E
R Ý J F C N O X U D R Ü M N
A Y V R M B L Z W L E N G B
Ç L X Y Q E A C T E Y I U E
O K T Ý A B R A G R ˋ Z S L I
R U H N A M W W G P M V Y K
S I Ş E N B E G Ý A N W A R
C X Q W D G F U A Q E F G Y
S P K R Y N U S U D M L E Q
X E P O C R S T X W D Q C H
```

APREL	AY
AWGUST	NOÝABR
KALENDAR	OKTÝABR
FEWRAL	ŞENBE
JUMA GÜNI	RUHNAM
ÝANWAR	ÝEKŞENBE
IÝUL	SIŞENBE
MART	ÇARŞENBE
MAGTYMGULY	HEPDE
DUŞENBE	ÝYL

8 - Energy

```
G B U C A D R O P O I E B F
I A U H Q I W O T M J L E O
R D I H Z V H K T C A E N T
I I S H A H K Z F O C K Z O
Ş Z A Ý E R A T A B M T I N
N E G O R D I G Ş E E R N H
O L T S G V D G E D V I T A
R Q K B G I T T M Y X K U P
T T Y L T D P L A M J K R A
K Y L Y L Y T A L W A A B L
E S A N A T Ç Y L Y K R I A
L E R K P N C Z A K G B N N
E F U E L E O J Q Y Q O A M
D A Ş K Y G U R Ş A W N N A
```

BATAREÝA	GIDROGEN
KARBON	SANATÇYLYK
DIZEL	MOTOR
ELEKTRIK	UCADRO
ELEKTRON	FOTON
GIRIŞ	HAPALANMA
DAŞKY GURŞAW	BUHAR
FUEL	TURBINA
BENZIN	ŞEMAL
ATYLYLYK	

9 - Archeology

```
A  M  G  I  J  Q  G  B  G  S  D  F  C  Y
S  N  A  P  B  P  Ö  A  Ö  N  Y  D  A  N
E  E  A  M  R  W  Z  H  W  Ä  R  R  N  Y
K  M  T  L  L  I  L  A  R  B  A  Ý  T  B
E  R  B  V  I  B  E  L  E  E  Z  Y  I  A
I  E  W  P  S  Z  G  A  L  L  A  L  K  D
O  H  Z  P  O  R  Ç  N  I  L  M  L  U  A
F  B  R  T  F  X  I  M  L  I  B  A  I  T
D  O  J  R  K  Y  S  A  I  O  O  R  T  H
V  B  O  E  E  Y  P  K  K  X  T  C  Y  A
N  V  W  P  C  G  I  C  A  E  R  J  K  N
K  K  D  S  Q  T  S  Ü  Ň  K  L  E  R  A
Z  Y  S  K  I  L  E  R  G  Z  S  T  B  D
X  H  Z  E  A  D  N  A  M  O  K  D  M  X
```

ANALIZ	SYR
ANTIKUITY	OBJECT
SÜŇKLER	RELIK
GÖWRELILIK	GÖZLEGÇI
NESIP	KOMANDA
ERMEN	YBADATHANA
BAHALANMAK	MAZARY
EKSPERT	NÄBELLI
FOSIL	ÝYLLAR

10 - Food #2

```
Ç T E O B S S A Ý O G U R T
I W I K A E P M A H Y H T B
G G R E L L Y L E L Q P J A
I N K P Y E W A U S Q D M R
T I I A K R B Q Z B E W F T
V X Ç N D I L Ü F P Y L G I
N V R A Ç Ş Y Z Ç E Ý E E Ç
S Z O N T E U Ü I I A L M O
U Z D A Q N R M Q M D Q T K
H H I B T D Z R C X G V S P
Ý U M U R T G A I K U H A D
B R O K K O L I F H B Q H N
E Z P A A Q S W F E W Z C U
Ş O K O L A T L N C L V O H
```

ALMA	MESELE
ARTIÇOK	BALYK
BANANA	ÜZÜM
BROKKOLI	HAM
SELERI	KIWI
ÇEÝE	MUŞDAK
ÇERRI	ÇIGIT
ÇIK	POMIDOR
ŞOKOLAT	BUGDAÝ
ÝUMURTGA	ÝOGURT

11 - Chemistry

```
H  T  J  N  D  A  G  R  A  M  C  K  K  W
I  L  E  X  U  C  M  Z  B  M  D  Y  I  A
B  R  O  M  Z  C  W  U  M  V  C  L  S  S
V  F  M  R  P  O  R  G  A  N  I  K  L  C
D  A  I  I  I  E  L  C  Q  X  B  U  O  A
U  A  U  P  X  N  R  Y  M  T  O  W  T  T
A  M  G  T  S  Y  L  A  T  A  K  U  A  O
L  C  I  U  A  K  D  I  T  M  M  S  N  M
K  M  D  H  A  Y  G  U  E  U  Z  R  E  A
A  E  R  U  M  Y  A  S  C  G  R  W  G  P
L  N  O  I  Q  Z  Z  D  L  A  G  A  I  P
I  Z  G  K  A  R  B  O  N  Y  D  O  S  L
N  I  E  E  L  E  K  T  R  O  N  R  K  M
E  M  N  A  T  Y  L  Y  L  Y  K  S  O  G
```

KISLOTA	GIDROGEN
ALKALINE	ION
ATOM	SUWUKLYK
KARBON	UCADRO
KATALYST	ORGANIK
HLORIN	OKSIGEN
ELEKTRON	DUZ
ENZIM	TEMPERATURA
GAZ	AGRAM
ATYLYLYK	

12 - Music

```
Y  H  K  V  O  K  A  L  D  U  Y  Y  D  H
E  R  A  Q  B  P  M  H  Y  U  Q  J  N  O
U  D  D  K  T  M  S  G  V  W  Y  Z  B  R
A  R  L  I  G  E  H  D  L  Y  M  V  L  G
Z  D  A  N  U  M  E  L  O  D  I  Ý  A  S
A  L  B  O  M  R  E  K  L  E  K  T  I  K
S  K  V  M  Y  Y  G  Z  A  C  E  M  O  S
O  F  L  R  R  H  D  B  A  G  Ş  Y  P  A
P  D  O  A  Y  A  F  Ý  Y  L  Q  W  E  Z
R  E  F  G  S  Ş  K  V  A  I  G  F  R  L
D  I  I  M  T  S  C  V  T  R  V  T  A  A
G  Q  T  Y  R  W  Y  Q  X  I  K  H  P  Ş
D  I  Y  M  W  F  W  K  J  K  R  N  N  Y
M  I  K  R  O  P  O  N  Y  I  V  V  B  K
```

ALBOM	SAZ
BALDAK	MUGT
HOR	OPERA
KLASSYKY	ŞAHYR
EKLEKTIK	ECAZGY
GARMONIK	YRYM
SAZLAŞYK	RITM
LIRIKI	AÝDYM
MELODIÝA	BAGŞY
MIKROPON	VOKAL

13 - Family

```
M L P A K U T Y Q M A Ý A L
T V N R U V W K G Y Z Y D O
W I B M E M H V Y Ý L L O A
A G T Y G Y X S C A Ý U G T
C O S E Y H I H K D S Ç A I
D A Ý Z A C S Y B R T A N X
B J E I I Q X L F P M G Y B
H W I S P Y O A M A M A J A
N M N U W M W O B G H L D B
L E N L A N R E T A P A F A
H J P F C T Ä T M Ç B R G B
J E V H Z C A U L O E A W A
X K I L E N E J J Y O R T B
F F C V A W G Y S G A Ç A A
```

ATA-BABA	AGTYGY
DAÝZA	ÄR
DOGAN	ENELIK
ÇAGA	EJE
ÇAGALAR	NEPHEW
GYSGAÇA	NIEÝS
GYZY	PATERNAL
ATA	UÝA
BABABABA	DAÝYM
MAMA	AÝAL

14 - Farm #1

```
T Ç B M K I Q N B P I K E J
E I K E M I G L E Ö S Ö K L
N G I O Z C Ç Y Ý V H P E B
E I Ş K W G E Ç I E A E R I
Ç T I A O P E O F Ş Ý K A Z
I O P Ý R H C R C E U P N O
R T N S K P R O Y K O F Ç N
K Y B P R O Z J A B M P Y D
G A L P S G A E T U V I L D
E R L P I J U T Q B B V Y L
Q M U F I Q W Q N F F F O K V
A P P T O H U M L A R A A J
X X S W W J S W T R F O D E
E P U E Z Q P P G A E G L K
```

EKERANÇYLYK	KAÝS
BEÝ	TENEÇIR
BIZON	SÖELGI
KALF	GEÇI
PIŞIK	HAÝ
ÇIK	PUL
KOW	AT
KROW	ÇIGIT
KÖPEK	TOHUMLAR
EŞEK	SUW

15 - Camping

```
V K R O P B A N N O Y S A Y
G O A I N S E K S I Ý A T Q
G M H B G Ü L K I P T P R V
V M U D I B T O K A Ý M A M
A A Ç E Ş N Y G N A Ý O K Y
A H E A Ü F K X Z F S K Y F
A D H X D H A Ý W A N L A R
G F V O V Y D F E Y A W Z W
A O C E S U R N C U N X P Z
Ç K O L N T E B I G A T H T
L H R Ö G T R B J S T I N D
A M Q G X V U T J D G J A M
R T H A T O S R R A Z S X W
K A G P U D N C E K A N O E
```

ADVENTURE	AW
HAÝWANLAR	INSEKSIÝA
KABIN	GÖLE
KANOE	KARTA
KOMPAS	AY
ÝANGYN	DÜŞ
TOKAÝ	TEBIGAT
GÜLKI	ROP
HAMMOK	ÇADYR
HAT	AGAÇLAR

16 - Algebra

```
J  Ý  N  Z  Q  B  S  O  U  G  S  Z  P  K
J  V  A  M  M  A  R  G  A  I  D  Y  Q  H
O  R  V  L  Y  T  O  A  S  Q  A  W  G  A
S  A  N  Y  A  I  L  R  Ü  D  G  R  A  F
S  Ş  O  L  B  N  Ç  A  M  E  S  E  L  E
K  I  A  E  F  I  Ö  E  V  Q  H  L  O  D
I  R  M  R  W  F  Z  N  P  E  W  C  N  A
R  I  G  Ö  B  N  Ü  I  E  N  E  A  T  A
T  W  F  Y  N  I  W  L  Ç  Ö  Z  M  K  L
A  É  A  Y  S  E  W  E  E  K  N  A  U  U
M  P  K  Y  B  G  K  G  V  P  K  R  X  M
H  D  T  X  D  L  A  E  B  Q  I  U  S  R
H  W  O  U  G  E  J  Ç  Ý  E  Q  G  K  O
K  W  R  C  X  T  L  W  A  R  B  S  F  F
```

DIAGRAMMA	SANY
GURAMA	ENE-ATA
GYSGAÇA	MESELE
FAKTOR	SIMÖNEKEÝ
ÝALAN	ÇÖZÜW
FORMULA	ÇÖZ
GRAF	EWIRIŞ
INFINIT	DÜRLI
LINEAR	NOL
MATRIKS	

17 - Numbers

```
Y H E E Q F M V R S J Ü Ç W
E B I R A D U L O E H L G Z
O V E D I N J I A K Ý N O L
D N U C S I K I E I D E F I
P T L A L T Y Y Q Z O E D M
P F D I K E R Z Y I K K S I
U K E X K M E Ö U K U Z I R
Ü Ç Ü N J I H W D E Z F R G
M U H K B Ä Ş Y W S Y Y B I
O G W I C V Q V T N N C B W
K D O K U Z C T S O J S X P
Q K J Z I M M Y J N Y T L A
K O B I W C I D W Q L F G C
G N A D O T Z K M A T U A D
```

ONLIK	VEDINJI
SEKIZ	ALTY
ON SEKIZ	ALTYNJY
BÄŞ	ON
DÖRT	ÜÇÜNJI
MAT	ÜÇ
DOKUZ	IKI
DOKUZYNJY	WIGRIMI
BIR	NOL
ÝEDI	

18 - Spices

```
K  I  L  R  A  G  W  A  N  I  L  L  A  Q
F  S  U  H  N  N  O  M  A  N  N  I  S  N
J  E  W  H  I  I  S  O  J  O  S  J  U  U
K  P  N  X  S  M  F  M  Y  R  X  Ý  W  T
O  Ö  R  N  E  U  R  A  F  F  R  Ü  R  M
Z  V  P  P  E  J  Q  D  P  A  E  S  P  E
M  T  X  E  I  L  H  R  N  Ş  G  N  G  G
O  D  A  Ň  Q  S  A  T  A  N  C  Q  A
P  A  P  R  I  K  A  K  A  C  I  R  Ü  K
F  E  N  U  G  R  E  K  G  D  G  R  M  S
S  M  I  C  L  N  R  O  A  D  U  Z  O  Y
F  U  S  G  R  S  M  Z  M  S  K  N  C  K
N  R  W  Y  U  B  C  K  P  X  S  D  D  D
Q  T  I  X  L  A  S  Ö  O  V  G  I  D  K
```

ANISE	TAGAM
AJY	GARLIK
KARDAMOM	GINGER
SINNAMON	NUTMEG
SÖOVGI	KÖPEŇ
KORIANDR	PAPRIKA
JUMIN	ŞAFRON
KÜRI	DUZ
FENNEL	SÜÝJI
FENUGREK	WANILLA

19 - Universe

```
G L G L U P O K S E L E T G
A A I O Q Q Y O G Ü N W R Ö
L T X Y N K M S U U A G Y R
A I X W A Ş W M B Z M B H N
K T H L E F Y I I S S J L I
T U A M L U W K S Z A A D Ş
I D R A S T E R O I D O Y P
K E E G A R A Ň K Y L Y K A
A O F P K L M K Ç Ö Z G Ü N
U I S E L E K Z O D I A K O
U M O N O R T S A C D C O R
A S M L O S C N E O N C E B
H O T H E M R A S Y R I O I
I O A S T R O N O M I Ý A T
```

ASTEROID	GONŞY
ASTRONOM	LATITUDE
ASTRONOMIÝA	AY
ATMOSFERA	ORBIT
KELESI	ASMAN
KOSMIK	GÜN
GARAŇKYLYK	ÇÖZGÜN
EON	TELESKOP
GALAKTIKA	GÖRNIŞ
HEMRASY	ZODIAK

20 - Mammals

```
P N P D L B N Ý Q Z E I K J
K O Q Ü E A P O L H D K C J
D A T Ý L L Y L U P O Ö B M
Z R N E S I D B T A M P D V
V B U G O N M A I U Ö E F A
C E Ý Y Ý A G R L N J K X L
X Z O Y G U H S K T E Y C S
I I G B E O Ý I I O K J N P
F H W D E I S P Z W E R I G
X J K G F A O M A Ş Ö F F T
Y J Y O E I W P A A K J L B
Q U U W Y M B E Z N Ü G E I
P I Ş I K O J K R U Z N D G
W Z T B L B T G O R I L L A
```

AÝY	GORILLA
BEAWER	AT
ÖKÜZ	KANGÝUÝ
DÜÝE	ÝOLBARS
PIŞIK	PUL
KOYOT	TOWŞAN
KÖPEK	GOÝUN
DELFIN	BALINA
TILKI	MÖJEK
GIREW	ZEBRA

21 - Fishing

```
H Z T X D M G W N I Q I Y D
J Ü Ý J E Ö C U B A Ý T D E
G G Ö L E W U S R T G I L L
S Ä C S U S I D A N O B F J
A S M N S Ü O A N S A G G L
B A T I O M W H E A W M E X
Y K S F I O P P K Z G D A K
R B A S Y M G A O X P R P P
L A W E R I Ý A K J O I A W
Y H O K E A N K U U F W H M
L U L U U A Z C H R K B L T
Y G Y S G A Ç A Ç L Y K E S
K A Z P L X I K K Y W X M F
R O G X M N R G S O B P A P
```

BAÝT
BASYM
KENAR
GÄMI
KOK
GURNAMA
GYSGAÇAÇLYK
FINS
GILL
HUK

JÜÝJE
GÖLE
OKEAN
SABYRLYLYK
AWERIÝA
MÖWSÜM
SUW
AGRAM
WIR

22 - Bees

```
G I Z C R P V U X G Q W F O
A Ý I S K E S N I Ü A S J Z
R M I L I Ç L E M L I P Y Z
O I N N E Z U L E T V F G W
S T O Q Q J P O Ü C R H O A
P E Ý D A L Y P E G A B W I
B W I S U L F J V V T D W W
A I S Y W H Q Y Q G Y M A V
Q M O M J A A F I R N Q X L
C E K D X K R B F Y L Q Z L
C S E M B D Z M I A Y W V L
T O Z D U R Y J Y T K V X J
Ö S Ü M L I K L E R A B D C
G Ü N C K V P D Y D Q T C U
```

PEÝDALY   PUL
GÜL   INSEKSIÝA
AIVRATYNLYK   ÖSÜMLIKLER
EKOSIÝON   POLEN
GÜLLER   TOZDURYJY
IÝMIT   SORAG
MIWE   ÇILIM
BAG   GÜN
HABITAT   SWARM
AIW   WAX

23 - Photography

```
G E S X Y Z F A F G T O Y P
P A R E G E L Ö K G A R M O
D Ý R Y R O Z Z Ň A S R Ç R
F I E A R G H I E H K K A T
R S L R Ň O I J R B A V R R
N I T U M K Y V F H M K Ç E
K Z R T T E Y S H A Ş N U T
M O E X K T V L Y Ş Y K W R
D P Ş E Q A P N Y I P A A K
V M Z T A M M U X K S Y E O
L O K S I R S E M O W Z U K
Q K V F V O O A R P P C V X
I U I E V F A M T A L Ň A R
W I S U A L N B Y I F I W X
```

GAR   ÇARÇUWA
KAMERA   YŞYK
REŇK   MAKSAT
KOMPOZISIÝA   ŞAHSY .ET
ŞERTLER   PORTRET
GARAŇKYLYK   KÖLEGE
AŇLATMA   MOWZUK
SERGI   TEXTURA
FORMAT   WISUAL

24 - Weather

```
G A E L A K I P O R T G G Y
Z Y E C I M L E H R M U U Y
W L Z F K Z D I P K T R R Ş
L E E Y Z H Z N M U G R Y Y
T N E U K F M G K A P I F K
H X R A L O P P B S T K T H
U D B B R A I N B O W A E P
N E U T W I N D R D F N M Y
D T R M H Q J A Ý A K E H M
E F B E A F C Ş Ü N R Ö G J
R S D N I N H V T R G T H D
O K Q O T H R N O O S N O M
H Y F S T E M P E T Q A T B
T E M P E R A T U R A R D Z
```

BREEZE

KLIMAT

GYZYK

GÖRNÜŞ

GURY ..

DUMAN

GURRIKAN

ICE

YŞYK

MONSOON

POLAR

RAINBOW

SKY

HEKAÝA

TEMPERATURA

THUNDER

TORNADO

TROPIKAL

WIND

25 - Adventure

```
B O K B O I Ş L E R B Y P X
N A W I G A S I Ý A R D R F
G Ş H T F H N J Y C V A R M
T Ö A W B T A H A Ý Y S J Ü
E Y Z T R H Ş N B K Z K O M
B Z M E L Ä D Y T A D A Ş K
I Y S Z L Y E U L T H M G I
G S Q Ä G L K E X R O U U N
A H F T P Z I Y F V W Y N Ç
T G W G N I K K L I P K L I
T A Ý Ý A R L Y K N L P Y L
H O W P S U Z L Y K Y I L I
G Ö R N Ü Ş E Z O C G K Y K
D O S T L A R F Y R G P K V
```

IŞLER	SYÝAHAT
GÖZELLIK	ŞATLYK
ŞANS	TEBIGAT
HOWPLY	NAWIGASIÝA
MAKSADY	TÄZE
KYNLYK	MÜMKINÇILIK
JOŞGUNLYLYK	TAÝÝARLYK
GÖRNÜŞ	HOWPSUZLYK
DOSTLAR	ADATY DÄL

26 - Sport

```
Ý Ü R E K D A M A R Y H B I
U R K X U B G J X P Q F B Ý
P A Y P J B P M T A S K A M
R L L L Y E S N A T R F Ş I
E A Y Y D M O A Q C J C A T
L R L N W A Ç A G S Y G R L
K O M E N D I Ý A L W U N E
S P A D E A E T A E Y I Y N
U S D E G P T U O Q I K K M
M G Y B R Ö B E R H I Z D E
L Ü Ç D Ü K L V X S O C S K
F Ý N P T Ň P R O G R A M J
M Ç M I O I S Ü Ň K L E R Z
M E T A B O L I K J O G Ä P
```

BAŞARNYK	MAKSAT
TÜRGEN	SAGLYK
BEDEN	JOGÄP
SÜŇKLER	IŇ KÖP ADAM
ÝÜREK-DAMAR	METABOLIK
KOMENDIÝA	MUSKLER
GYSGAÇA	IÝMITLENMEK
TANS	PROGRAM
BERHIZ	SPORALAR
ÇYDAMLYLYK	GÜÝÇ

27 - Circus

```
Ý M Y R Q M E P U L W D J J
C O B Q P U S Z G R S J H A
T Y L C N S H E Ň A Q U A D
M F O B P I M K A L N O Ý Y
K J I O A K U R L N D Q W G
N C U N T R T Ö P O R A A Ö
R A G G J I S G A L U W N Ý
X L J L G E O S G A G N L M
B I L I K L K G P B W C A R
Y Y H K W B E Ç A D Y R R N
A K R O B A T R O T K E P S
P A R A D E S S I O Z L I P
D J A D Y G Ö Ý L I K I A A
B V M L D M T S L Y M H Z O
```

AKROBAT	PUL
HAÝWANLAR	MUSIK
BALONLAR	PARADE
KLOUN	GÖRKEZ
KOSTUM	SPEKTOR
JUGGLER	ÇADYR
ÝOLBARS	BILIK
JADYGÖÝLIK	GAPLAŇ
JADYGÖÝ	HILE

28 - Geology

```
K M I N E R A L A R K E W B
A I E O P L F H M E O R U E
L I S O F L G E S Z R O L R
T C E L R Q A D L Ý A Z K S
A A Ş W O Z N T G E L I A P
G L A V A T L D E G L Ý N O
Z U D V H T A G I O R A H C
K O N T I N E N T A R T E R
K Y X A L R Y M T P A D P B
R W T Q R E Z S X R L W M W
W U A K Z W T D I J K V X D
E M E R R A L K Y Z Y G N K
N A F E S K B J Ý I S L A K
S T A L A K T I T E X E C M
```

KISLOTA
KALSIÝ
KAWERN
KONTINENT
KORAL
GYZYKLAR
SYKLAR
ARTER
EROZIÝA
FOSIL

GEÝZER
LAVA
GATLAK
MINERALAR
PLATEO
KWARS
DUZ
STALAKTIT
DAŞ
WULKAN

29 - House

```
R U V O K L Q G O B F M Z J
W A L L G A P Y C Y I W P L
L R Ü Q L G Z H J H Q E E X
Y Y G K I T T A Ç A G S Y G
W Ç H H I V K C Y E N D J C
G A R A Ş T U N B W F U A S
L K B U A K Ç R A E A Ş R N
V G A T O Ç A E G Z K R A B
T R J Ý M S A G N S O O G Z
V F W H S A Z R S F J O V F
W K P W S Ý X N Y A A F W F
X C O S T N M J G L K I R K
W T E F X A N A H P A T I K
Ö Ý G O Ş L A R Y W P R A A
```

ATTIK	AÇARYLAR
GARAŞ	KITÇEN
GYSGAÇA	ÇYRA
GAPY	KITAPHANA
KAÝS	AÝNA
OJAK	ROOF
GÜL	OTAG
ÖÝ GOŞLARY	DUŞ
GARAJY	WALL
BAG	EWEZ

30 - Physics

```
U  N  I  V  E  R  S  A  L  B  U  F  M  Z
U  C  I  Y  G  M  O  T  A  Ö  C  O  E  I
T  A  D  X  F  A  N  F  A  L  A  R  X  E
B  I  S  K  U  P  T  E  Y  Ü  D  M  A  E
G  H  Z  A  G  R  S  N  L  M  R  U  N  M
D  Y  K  Y  Z  L  Y  K  A  Z  O  L  I  A
M  O  T  O  R  D  C  E  S  Ş  I  A  K  G
H  I  M  I  Ý  A  S  X  S  A  Y  T  A  N
K  A  O  S  L  Y  K  Q  A  M  R  K  S  E
E  L  E  K  T  R  O  N  M  Y  G  Y  Ý  T
M  O  L  E  K  U  L  Ý  A  R  P  H  L  I
T  E  R  J  I  M  E  K  O  B  D  W  O  Z
Z  I  Y  R  A  O  Q  Y  J  K  W  Y  B  M
G  E  K  R  G  Z  M  Z  Q  S  D  U  F  K
```

TIZLENME	MAGNETIZM
ATOM	MASSALY
KAOSLYK	MEXANIKA
HIMIÝA	MOLEKULÝAR
DYKYZLYK	UCADRO
ELEKTRON	BÖLÜM
MOTOR	GATNAŞYK
FORMULA	TIZ
ÝYGYM	UNIVERSAL
GAZ	TERJIME

31 - Dance

```
S  G  K  O  F  G  L  Q  A  K  D  H  H  A
U  Y  I  Ö  K  B  A  L  K  R  J  O  U  K
R  S  S  X  Ň  F  U  P  I  Z  T  R  D  A
A  G  U  Q  S  L  S  N  Q  W  E  E  S  D
T  A  M  L  C  T  I  Y  I  K  Ý  O  Ö  E
Z  Ç  E  P  Y  V  W  Q  B  L  I  G  W  M
Ş  A  D  T  A  M  Z  Y  H  A  N  R  D  I
I  G  N  S  Q  Y  Q  G  R  S  E  A  A  Ý
K  N  B  Ý  V  R  O  Ý  Q  S  D  F  L  A
C  K  P  E  B  Y  E  U  W  Y  E  I  O  P
F  O  C  R  D  M  K  D  X  K  M  Ý  R  E
G  R  A  C  E  E  Q  C  G  Y  J  A  X  M
M  U  K  W  Q  H  N  Ş  A  T  L  Y  K  R
O  V  Y  C  Y  S  V  K  T  K  U  M  D  J
```

AKADEMIÝA	ŞATLYK
ART	KÖŇLI
BEDEN	MUSIK
HOREOGRAFIÝA	HYZMATDAŞ
KLASSYKY	SURAT
MEDENIÝET	REÝS
DUÝGY	YRYM
GYSGAÇA	SÖWDA
GRACE	WISUAL

32 - Colors

```
O W Ç G V Q U C C N E G X Q
G L C Ý U L D R F T B Y O Q
J A R K A T N E G A M Z G J
K Y R A S N A U V G E Y A A
Y I Ü H Q C C U L L P L R S
Y S P I V L B G P O Y Y A Y
F Ç E V I O L E T Ň N Ş Ş G
F U R B E Ý J K S O L A W F
V F Ü B K L W I I U V Ý A T
Q K P Q I I K U F U S H Z Y
F W S E Ý D I Ý A N G N U Z
H P V X R L F Y A K Ý Ç R G
H M V I C Z J Y P V Ö N E G
O Z W H K Y H J Y D G G U S
```

AZURE	MAGENTA
BEÝJ	OŇOLGA
GAR	PEMBE
GÖK	PÜRE-PÜR
GARAŞ	GYZYL
ÇYAN	SEÝDIÝA
FUÇSIYA	VIOLET
ÝAŞYL	AK
ÇYK	SARYK

33 - Shapes

```
B E J F X D Q E S P I L E K
U Z R K U E B L M R E A A U
R T A L O B R E P I G V R B
Ç X G M T H G D K Z F O Ç D
P A R A T T A H R M H E F Ä
Z O H W R F Ý H G A F G D B
I B L Y X I D K N Ö Z R R I
J K E I E M L E K K R I M Ň
U V I J G N A L Q J X N H O
I F N N K O R L I D H T Ü M
K M T Ü J Z N E E I G C L Ş
K M C Ç L I P Ý H A M I D I
O W V Ü A U M W C F V O C P
N Q Y R U K Y Y H S F L X O
```

ARÇ	HAT
DÄBIŇ	OVAL
KON	POLIGON
BURÇ	PRIZMA
KUB	PÝHAMIDI
EGRI	GÖRNÜŞ
KELLE	TARAP
GAÝDLAR	IKINJI
ELIPSE	ÜÇÜNJI
GIPERBOLA	

34 - Scientific Disciplines

```
R Y L B Z O L O G I A M A E
G X A K I N A X E M I Y K K
F A Ý I G O L O N U M M I O
D R B O A M H M I R K C N L
B H Q G L Z Z I T H S C A O
D I N G U I W G M H O N T G
I J O E V P Q E X I H J O I
L E D L C A E Z V F Ý Z B Ý
L M R L O A Ý I M O T A N A
E G Q J Ý G O L A R E N I M
R Y C Y A Ý I G O L O E G O
C E C H J X B Ý Z C F H F E
I T R I M R L D A Ý I M I H
N E W R O L O G I Ý A J Z G
```

ANATOMIÝA	IMMUNOLOGIÝA
BIOHIMIÝA	DILLER
BIOLOGIÝA	MEXANIKA
BOTANIKA	MINERALOGÝ
HIMIÝA	NEWROLOGIÝA
EKOLOGIÝA	JEMGY .ET
GEOLOGIÝA	ZOLOGI .A

35 - Science

```
G M S Ö B Ö L Ü M L E R F U
U A R S E H J L M I T C A E
Z G U Ü H I M I Ý A E U K G
R L F M M U Y L U J S T F
A U R L G Y I A M A R U G O
L M U I R L Q N U I I L Z S
A A L K A Y V Ç E O B X T I
L T T L W G I O A R E C H L
U L A E I A T O M K A X M M
K A G R T A M I L K L L X V
E R I L Y F I Z I K A A A D
L A B O R A T O R I Ý A M R
O U E E W O L Ý U S I Ý A A
M O T U K W M F T Y B D Y Q
```

ATOM
HIMIÝA
KLIMAT
MAGLUMATLAR
EWOLÝUSIÝA
TEJRIBE
FAKT
FOSIL
GRAWITY
ÇAKLAMA

LABORATORIÝA
USUL
MINERALAR
MOLEKULALAR
TEBIGAT
GURAMA
BÖLÜMLER
FIZIKA
ÖSÜMLIKLER
YLYM

36 - Beauty

```
Z G H R M A K A L A N Ý A S
W R H Y Ö N Ü M L E R X L T
B A A D Z Y F V Z F V L G Y
L O J G O M A A U A Q A Y L
A Z G Y C L A X E I X R S I
K N D S X Y U T Z K G A G S
I E Ç A R M O Q L Y T K A T
T G L Ş A M P O O A Y S Ç Y
E O F L O W A D A N R A A I
M T V J E R E Ň K D J M H V
S O W Q Q L S M K L E C H Z
O F D U M R E Y C R T R K H
K G R A C E V R U I J K I U
W V A R O W A D A N L Y K D
```

ÇARM	AÝNA
REŇK	FOTOGEN
KOSMETIKA	ÖNÜMLER
KELLELER	YLM
OWADANLYK	GYSGAÇA
OWADAN	HYZMATLAR
YS	ŞAMPOO
GRACE	DERI
MAKALA	SYGDYR
MASKARA	STYLIST

37 - Clothes

```
N A I N Z U C R Y T E K A J
G A R S A N D A L L A R S G
A D A E W E W R E Ý T H K Ö
Ý O L H P T P B A L A K A R
O M A K M P A G K A Ý A R N
B F M L S D L Ž C E B L F Ü
B S A E R P T Y A Z U E H Ş
T Z J T G A O K E N Ý Ö K H
L X A Ý A I Q H Q O R M Q W
G U P E Y G N O Z R W R H R
I K M B O T Z E K P K M H Z
N E C F P A J A Ş A V G W T
R N L F K Ö Z V F I Q C X I
H Y I R Y S Z I J R K E T E
```

APRON	EWEWREÝ
BEÝTEL	BOÝAG
GAR	PAJAMALAR
GÖRNÜŞ	BALAK
PALTO	SANDALLAR
EGIN-EŞIK	SKARF
MODA	KÖÝNEK
HAT	AÝAKGAP
JAKET	ETEK
ŽANR	SÖATGI

38 - Ethics

```
H F S V O L S P P R R O E B
M O I A M N V Ä Ä E A P M Z
E P R L B K Z H K A S T A K
R A G M O Y P I L L A I S Y
T H O Y A S R M I I L M L L
E F E Ş K T O L K Z L I A Ş
B W W R R V G F Y M Y Z H A
E J L A P Y Z O I L K M A D
T O L G U N M A K Ý Y J T T
M Ä H I R L I L I K A K U A
Q I N D I V I D U A L I Z M
Q A D A M Z A T Q S B K T Z
D I P L O M A T I K Z Q J Y
L Q I A L T R U I Z M Z V H
```

ALTRUIZM	OPTIMIZM
GARŞY	SABYRLYLYK
HYZMATDAŞLYK	FILOSOFIÝA
MERTEBE	RASALLYK
DIPLOMATIK	REALIZM
PÄKLIK	MASLAHAT
ADAMZAT	HORMAT
INDIVIDUALIZM	TOLGUNMAK
MÄHIRLILIK	PÄHIM

39 - Insects

```
L K S I K A D A S X Q L E F
O Z E N A N B U G D Y E F L
K G D W Y H R G E G K S W E
U W X D M S C L X U A A V Ý
S L G R A S S H O P P E R A
T W A S P H I G U Z U X Y E
A I I D K O Y T N A R N U Q
G P Q Ş N R A L N U G O B T
A V H P R N Y F I A L P F E
R S J I H E K R R L A Z V R
A H I Z D T C H H T R D Y M
Ş D I J H O R A Z Ý W M E I
Y M M E J E L X G E A G C T
S Ö T E R G I D B B B E Ý S
```

ANT
APHID
BEÝ
BEÝTLA
SÖTERGI
SIKADA
HORAZ
GARAŞY
FLEÝA
GRASSHOPPER

HORNET
ZENANBUG
LARWA
LOKUST
ANTIS
BOGUNLAR
EJE
TERMIT
WASP
IŞ

40 - Astronomy

```
M T Y A S T R O N A W T X G
W E A L U B E N D F J Z C Ö
C K T S U P E R N O W A K Z
R K E E R A D I A S I Ý A E
F O N I O P K A I D O Z A G
K R A M A R J S O M S O K Ç
A P L Z Y J R T E P K M I I
R S P M T Ş M R E Ý O Z T L
M K M M Y P Ü O S V N I K I
B B H A Y I C N H E E D A K
V S D M N L O O R W W R L P
Z E J O H K S M U Ö E A A G
U U S A T E L L I T G V G O
A S T E R O I D W V B H A K
```

ASTEROID	AY
ASTRONAWT	NEBULA
ASTRONOM	GÖZEGÇILIK
GÖRNÜŞ	PLANETA
KOSMOS	RADIASIÝA
ÝER	ROKKET
EKLIP	SATELLIT
EWENOKS	ASMAN
GALAKTIKA	SUPERNOWA
METEOR	ZODIAK

41 - Health and Wellness #2

```
K A P H O I K K A L L E R G
E K A R H Ý S A E N M J A A
X E H U O M I A L S F H G Ý
G S E N E I G Y G O E V R I
E E M T N T J W X L R L A M
N L A I T L O J K P Y I M O
E H S R Q E W T X Z B K Ý T
T A S Ş Ü N R Ö G G G A N A
I N A J O M J E P A F Ç I N
K A Ž D D E G X X Ý K A M A
A L O C N K I J F G Y G A T
Z A B E R H I Z B Y B S T S
N R M L E N E R G I A Y I E
I N F E K S I Y A J K G W C
```

ALLERG	SAGLYK
ANATOMIÝA	KESELHANALAR
GÖRNÜŞ	GYGIENE
GAN	INFEKSIYA
KALORIÝA	MASSAŽ
GYSGAÇA	IÝMITLENMEK
BERHIZ	GAÝGY
KESEL	WITAMIN
ENERGI .A	AGRAM
GENETIKA	

42 - Time

```
C V C F Y E Q H Y V H E Z U
F P H S O J P Y I L S C P Y
K A L E N D A R I T R E O L
Y M P G Ü Ý Z P K O I J A L
L S I U G Y N P N L Z I X Y
L A C N B L O O G E Ä G M K
Y G Q Ü U P S Y O F H H E Y
Ý A I G X D F Z Ö Ň V E R F
N T G U X R A L T Z U P K I
O Q S B A Y P A K I Q D E R
A I R K I B F R G F Z E Z G
H A J O N N D W O V R D D G
J T C Ý H C Z A K E J L E G
S U L R O D R B Z O V A S N
```

YZLAR	MINUDA
UYLLYK	AY
ÖŇ	ERTIR
KALENDAR	GIJE
MERKEZ	ÝOK
GÜN	HÄZIR
ONÝYLLYK	TIZDEN
IRKI	BU GÜN
GELJEK	HEPDE
SAGAT	ÝYL

43 - Buildings

```
K E S E L H A N A L A R D G
C X F U T N Q T Ý C A W I Ö
L X K T F S S L E A E A N Z
B Z F B L T P Y Z A L Ý U E
W A D O W A Z E U C T I J G
B Ö L Ü M D D A M U S R K Ç
O A N Y B I T I V Q A O I I
W P A C F O B I Ň F K T N L
K A B I N N R A B I P A O I
M E K D E B Y G R H R R Ç K
S U P E R M A R K E T O A M
M Y H M A N H A N A B B D A
V N K Q A N A H K A T A Y U
E I L Ç I H A N A P W L R Z
```

BÖLÜM	LABORATORIÝA
BARN	MUZEÝ
KABIN	GÖZEGÇILIK
KASTLE	MEKDEB
KINO	STADION
ILÇIHANA	SUPERMARKET
ZAWOD	ÇADYR
KESELHANALAR	TEATR
YATAKHANA	DIŇI
MYHMANHANA	

44 - Philanthropy

```
P S A D A K A L A R J M S S
Q R A L T A S K A M R B U L
R A O E M H H X W S S E T V
F L U G F Ş A U O Y F R O M
L T L S R A L A G A Ç M P I
T K L G U A K E R E G E A S
A A W E I M M F M S J K R S
Z T R F R A P M O A R Y L I
M N D Y O L Ä K A N Y J A O
A O S M H I K N V L D V R N
D K E U U Ý L R S L A L B B
A X D M K E I Q T O Y R A C
Q E F U U B K R O G Y Y R R
J E M G Y Ý E T A G A N E S
```

SADAKALAR	TARYH
ÇAGALAR	PÄKLIK
JEMGYÝET	ADAMZAT
KONTAKTLAR	MISSION
BERMEK	GEREK
MALIÝE	HALK
FONDLAR	PROGRAMMALAR
UMUMY	SENAGAT
MAKSATLAR	YOUAŞ
TOPARLAR	

45 - Gardening

```
O  W  V  N  A  C  T  O  P  R  A  K  F  K
T  R  G  Ü  L  D  R  Z  E  S  P  Y  O  L
O  E  Ç  Q  W  C  U  Z  O  N  A  L  L  I
H  N  D  A  J  K  U  B  D  H  H  G  I  M
U  I  I  S  R  X  C  V  I  H  F  Y  Ý  A
M  T  K  O  B  D  K  P  C  E  G  Ç  A  T
L  N  I  Ý  I  L  Ý  Ä  N  Ý  E  R  Ž  S
A  O  T  I  B  R  U  I  J  M  L  D  X  O
R  K  O  T  G  O  X  Y  G  W  M  K  E  P
Z  U  Z  K  X  H  T  N  M  Ü  S  W  Ö  M
C  N  K  N  F  T  H  A  D  V  F  U  N  O
Y  T  E  O  U  X  R  X  N  F  I  S  H  K
Ý  A  P  R  A  K  T  E  X  I  Y  V  N  Q
H  O  Z  K  H  H  A  L  D  G  K  R  Z  X
```

GÜL	FOLIÝAŽ
BOTANIK	HOZ
BUKJA	ÝAPRAK
KLIMAT	ÇYGLYK
KOMPOST	ORÇARD
KONTINER	MÖWSÜM
HAPA	TOHUMLAR
IÝILÝÄN ÝER	TOPRAK
EKZOTIK	SUW

46 - Herbalism

```
M A R J O R A M F Y W K K M
M Z A W O D O P K E A U V E
A R O M A T I K E I N I V F
I E N A X S F M R Ý I N G T
N D A G M R B P T P D E E F
G N G A T I D Y G A B A G L
R E E T Q N B R Q R L H L K
E W R R L Y Ş A Ý S E V Ü Y
D A O C X R A M S Y T E G N
I L M O N T J Y K I L R A G
E Q L X H H U Z C R L U G O
N O R F A Ş N O G A R R A T
T R V N E N U R C T X T Y E
K U L I N A R Y Q X T O P I
```

AROMATIK	INGREDIENT
BASIL	LAWENDER
PEÝDALY	MARJORAM
KULINARY	MONT
FENNEL	OREGANO
TAGAM	PARSY
GÜL	ZAWOD
BAG	ROZYMARY
GARLIK	ŞAFRON
ÝAŞYL	TARRAGON

47 - Vehicles

```
B U S Z E N Y L T A Ș W A N
K X C Y G I R X T M E R S J
Y Y K U P R P P N B L S F M
T U X W P N Q K A U B Y M O
T Y P U I L L E W L E H D T
I R R E F J R Ý A A O C W O
W O A N R H A R R T A I W R
Ș R M K A J F I A O R T E M
Ü E A R T H T T K R L A X U
N T E C G O U K R I T E Ç S
R O K K E T R I R Ý Z U A U
Ö K H T U R J E V A G J G L
G S N A B I K Y C L E G A Y
T A K S I M Ä G P C B L H B
```

UÇAR	RAFT
AMBULATORIÝA	ROKKET
BIKYCLE	SKOTER
GÄMI	ŞATLYN
BUS	METRO
CAR	TAKSI
KARAWAN	TIRÝEK
FERRI	TRAKTOR
HELWEL	GÖRNÜŞ
MOTOR	WAN

48 - Flowers

```
T D U P J P N H Q Z G O J T
M A G N O L I Ý A Y Ü R F N
L D A N D E L I O N N Ç R R
B A J Ü N Z G V F O E I H E
H U W G K G Y S C E B D S Y
N I K E F Ü Z A A P A N R Y
Y S B J N L Y V B I K A Ý L
E D L I A D K V K L A B G U
S D H L S U E C C U R G Z P
L I L Ý A K N R Q T N A M O
A Y I R E M U L P E O B T P
W V D C N I M S A Ý E K P B
G G J P S D B Y Q O L T Y K
V C T H G V A J P E T E K K
```

BUKJA

GYZYK

GÜN

DANDELION

BAGBAN

HIBISKUS

ÝASMIN

LAWENDER

LÝAK

LILÝA

MAGNOLIÝA

ORÇID

PEONY

PETEK

PLUMERIYA

POPULY

GÜL

GÜNEBAKAR

TULIP

49 - Health and Wellness #1

```
R O D G Q F T E A X B S C I
B S R Ö A N X T Ç N E P G M
S K T A W R S Q L S J S H L
D E R I L L Ş O Y X E F T V
I L M K I N E Y K R R H A O
N F G A D K O T X T G B Q S
D E F M O Y E M B T I B A H
U R J R K L N E R W E S K K
S Q B A T N V K V O N F I B
U K O F O A E Y Y Z G Y N Q
R D Ý G R M U S K L E R I R
I N A Ý I R E T K A B P L F
W R R U I E P I C S H D K Z
D Ö W Ü K D S Ü Ň K L E R J
```

INDUS	DERMANLYK
BAKTERIÝA	MUSKLER
SÜŇKLER	NERWES
KLINIKA	FARMAKI .A
DOKTOR	REFLEKS
DÖWÜK	GARŞY
HABIT	DERI
BOÝ	BEJERGI
GORMONLAR	DÖWLET
AÇLYK	WIRUS

50 - Town

```
H M S D Y L D L Z B P E V M
O E U T N R Y O R T A E T U
W K H E A K I N I L K N E Z
A D M T K D E I B F H I K E
M E W I Ü F I K L A U T R Ý
E B K S D K R O O Z Z N A K
N E P R P Z H A N N S A M I
Z E M E A D Ü K A N G R R T
I L P W T J P R T W Y O E A
L A F I I R E L A G R T P P
I P O N K Y Y Ü B U H S U H
E O A U C T C G G Q O E S A
F A R M A K I A Z Z F R C N
M Y H M A N H A N A P Q W A
```

HOWA MENZILI
BANK
KITAP DÜKANY
KINO
KLINIKA
GÜL
GALERI
MYHMANHANA
KITAPHANA
BAZAR

MUZEÝ
FARMAKI .A
RESTORAN
MEKDEB
STADION
DÜKAN
SUPERMARKET
TEATR
UNIWERSITET
ZOO

51 - Antarctica

```
B C D A Ş K Y G U R Ş A W J
A D A L A R A L K U L Z U B
H R S M Ý G Ö Z L E G Ç I G
H K U N I M E J Ş Y R G K U
W O K T F W I P Ü L Y Y O Ş
I N T S A I U G N Y L Z R L
B T V Y R R C S R M V L S A
D I I L G S E Ö A M A U R
V N H J O K E P G M S R W F
J E C E E U V Z M X E I L T
A N A H G A R O G E K Y Ý B
C T N J F B A Ý V K T R N A
T O P O G R A F I Ý A X D S
P E N I N S U L A K V L A H
```

BAÝ	ICE
GUŞLAR	ADALAR
GYZLAR	MIGRASIÝA
GORAGHANA	PENINSULA
KONTINENT	GÖZLEGÇI
KOW	ROKI
DAŞKY GURŞAW	YLYM
GÖRNÜŞ	TEMPERATURA
GEOGRAFIÝA	TOPOGRAFIÝA
BUZLUKLAR	SUW

52 - Ballet

```
Q L G M X T R E L K S U M Ö
N Q Y K U G O W C M O M H W
H P L I T S T A G N U S V R
N A Y L G Ý I D G J F C F E
D N M R Q E Z K Ü R H P U N
S I E E J R O T Ý Y R Y M M
Z R Ň W V B P F Ç I L D K E
R E H L R M M N H N S P T K
U L O E E K O D A L K Y Ş E
H A R A H M K O R K E S T R
B B T Q X U E T E R J I M E
G Y S G A Ç A K P B J S U G
M I Ş L I K L E R Z H P Q O
T A N S Ç Y L A R D Z D Q O
```

ALKYŞ	GÜÝÇ
SUNGAT	MUSKLER
DIŇLEMEK	MUSIK
BALERINA	ORKESTR
KOMPOZITOR	TERJIME
TANSÇYLAR	REÝS
GYSGAÇA	YRYM
ELWERLIK	ÖWRENMEK
GEREK	IŞLIKLER

53 - Fashion

```
G E C R M M M K K U A P P H
I E C J S S R P K H S E E Ä
M Z Ý I Q M K Q E Y Y S Ý Z
I Z T I N A D A W O L P D I
N X T C M U S V T D L Ä A R
I B B D D I S Y S R Y L L K
M U K Y L Ş A G K A N L Y I
A G I Q C L V A A K P I G Z
L O T D P I S L Ç S M K W A
I W U Ü V K I R B A F D K M
S Y B G R L F W U M G R E A
T G X L I E L E Ý Ç E S V N
T U Y E A R U T X E T D Y I
D N E R T Z V B A E A P A G
```

GOWY	MINIMALIST
BUTIK	HÄZIRKI ZAMAN
DÜGLER	PESPÄLLIK
GEÝIM	ASYLLY
OWADAN	NUSGA
NAKGAŞLYK	PEÝDALY
GYSGAÇA	IŞLIKLER
FABRIK	TEXTURA
LEÝÇE	TREND

54 - Human Body

```
K Y X H Ý B E C A I T E M I
E G I N Ü E Ç Z E G A N F Q
E I H B R Ý M Y I A E L R M
A X F J E N U D N Ý A W L E
Ý U I V K I S N V O Z N Y J
A P A A Y J N L J B Z B E Ý
K G N S X G K H N O A Q Z Ü
B I K A Q S U N M T I O T J
C K L O T S J L Ş A E T Y T
Z S E K K A M R A B U R U N
S Ü Ň K L E R B B K D E R I
M F C Z P U A G G G C P A P
M Q F A M Z X S Z H P O V T
H E Y I L Z L H P Z W A N Y
```

ANKLE
GAN
SÜŇKLER
BEÝNI
ÇYN
GULAK
ELWAÝ
ACÜZ
BARMAK
EL

BAŞ
ÝÜREK
JÜÝJE
DYZ
AÝAK
AY
BOÝAG
BURUN
EGIN
DERI

55 - Musical Instruments

```
D P E U M P Ý N I Ý A I T A
N R T B K A B A S Y M Ç I M
N A U O L B N S F G I T A R
K G L M A M O D E Q S R P Y
U Q F B R I F J O G I L E D
G K G R N R A T B L B B R M
W U B W E A S D O R I D K A
I O R W T M K H C P A N U T
O F L A H D A B A N J O S R
L W D L M T S N Q H Z B S O
I W S R A A Z U H D W I I M
N D V V U Z N F D W D H O B
Q N O N Y O L I P B A P N O
E H R G O N G Ç E L L O T N
```

BANJO	MANDOLIN
BASYM	MARIMBA
ÇELLO	OBOE
ÇIM	PERKUSSION
KLARNET	PÝNIÝA
DRUM	SAKSAFON
FLUTE	TAMDYR
GONG	TROMBON
GITAR	GURAMA
GARP	WIOLIN

56 - Fruit

```
A G A Ý A P A P N M N Q O E
V V P Y R R E B P S A R K T
O R R N I R A T K E N N A A
K A I Ü Z Ü M U K N O Z G J
A N K K G R L N X Ä M K R O
D A O G D H A O R D I D V K
O N T M V X A K D R L B Q F
R A F E U C A O V Ü X T M R
J S W H Z K O K Z D G F U J
U C Q L O X I R R E Ç I V X
A U B E R R I W P E Ç G N B
C T B M A O U N I U A W N A
B A N A N A V Y M G Q H S G
G U A W A B T C C L F Z C F
```

ALMA	KIWI
APRIKOT	LIMON
AVOKADO	MANGO
BANANA	MELHEM
BERRI	NEKTARIN
ÇERRI	PAPAÝA
KOKONUT	PEÇ
FIG	DÜRDÄNE
ÜZÜM	ANANAS
GUAWA	RASPBERRY

57 - Engineering

```
G  I  D  I  A  G  R  A  M  M  A  D  H  D
Z  Ö  Ş  P  L  S  E  M  E  U  T  E  A  K
H  M  R  L  L  E  W  I  L  E  R  G  S  J
J  C  O  N  I  P  H  O  I  W  Y  I  A  E
A  K  Ş  T  Ü  K  U  L  Ň  U  Ç  Ş  P  N
D  V  M  K  O  Ş  L  F  T  I  W  M  L  E
O  G  Ü  Ý  Ç  R  M  E  V  Z  G  Ä  A  R
M  Z  R  I  Q  X  N  S  R  A  E  G  M  G
S  U  W  U  K  L  Y  K  U  U  C  U  A  I
T  Q  Ö  V  K  Y  Ş  U  L  R  U  G  D  A
O  A  G  D  O  W  A  X  Y  F  M  E  I  L
I  B  E  A  I  A  M  A  R  U  G  Ç  Z  E
D  U  R  N  U  K  L  Y  L  Y  K  L  E  Z
Z  H  U  U  I  S  N  C  P  Y  X  Ö  L  N
```

IŞLIKLER	GEARS
AKŞ	LEWILER
HASAPLAMA	SUWUKLYK
GURLUŞYK	MAŞYN
ÇUŇLUK	ÖLÇEG
DIAGRAMMA	MOTOR
GÖWRÜM	GÖRNÜŞ
DIZEL	DURNUKLYLYK
DEGIŞMÄ	GÜÝÇ
ENERGI .A	GURAMA

58 - Kitchen

```
F N B B R I G X E N X Z B N
P O N O K Y P G T E V M I A
Y R R E W Y B R U D O T L P
J P E K J L O D J O V A E K
Y A L M L S N L U E K L N I
D F K A L A U Q G T X P L N
A T P E S E R E Z E R F E K
W I O L O I E O V L A L R Ä
O C Ç I Q G G U N T B S A S
S V T P W U N Y Q T K P L E
D L E Z I U Ü K P E M I Z L
S Z U N A U S A W K J C Y E
I Ý M I T G R I L L A E G R
B E B M N G S G U Y R S V Z
```

APRON	KETTLE
BOWL	BILENLER
ÇOPKLER	LAL
KÄSELER	NAPKIN
IÝMIT	OVEN
FORKLAR	RESEPT
FREZER	SOWADYJY
GRILL	SPICES
JAR	SÜNGER
JUG	GYZLAR

59 - Government

```
D G U N S P A Q Y L P U G Q
H N N Q Y A N D B K O J R O
K I N N M R I X A Y M L A Q
J A G A B A O Y R L I F Ý Y
B X N H O H X F T T A H A Z
M P O U L A W G E A D T T R
S Ö Z N N T E Ý Y Z A K L A
E D Z T E L W Ö D A N W Y Ý
J E D E L Y D E Ň L I K K A
I I D Y H K I T I L O P M T
Q P C Z W S Ý O L B A Ş Ç Y
K O N S T I T U S I Ý A H T
C G H A M I L L I V J B F E
G A R A Ş S Y Z L Y K D N T
```

RAÝATLYK
RAÝAT
KONSTITUSIÝA
JEDEL
ETRABY
DEŇLIK
GARAŞSYZLYK
KAZYÝET
ADALAT
KANUN

ÝOLBAŞÇY
AZATLYK
AY
MILLI
PARAHATLYK
POLITIK
SÖZ
DÖWLET
SYMBOL

60 - Art Supplies

```
K  I  L  I  J  I  D  E  R  Ö  D  G  S  K
S  A  E  D  I  E  N  A  M  I  A  B  K  A
B  I  M  L  E  S  A  E  A  Y  A  Y  T  G
V  R  H  E  W  L  G  A  Ý  O  B  H  Z  Y
W  C  J  W  R  A  L  M  A  L  A  G  C  Z
Y  K  N  T  T  A  U  F  H  W  U  S  G  R
R  B  Y  E  R  Ý  E  L  K  Y  E  K  L
I  R  V  J  A  K  R  Y  L  I  K  Ý  U  A
R  E  Ň  K  L  E  R  R  Y  V  D  Ý  L  I
E  C  T  M  W  J  L  N  H  Y  J  Ä  L  P
L  U  W  B  U  V  N  P  X  H  D  S  X  B
Ş  Q  B  Z  S  O  E  U  U  I  I  P  B  Y
İ  F  T  F  C  G  T  E  I  I  N  G  I  W
B  Y  R  L  G  F  R  X  P  G  L  K  P  S
```

AKRYLIK	GLUÝ
BIŞLER	IDEAS
KAMERA	INK
CHAIR	ÝAG
KLEÝ	KAGYZ
REŇKLER	GALAMLAR
DÖREDIJILIK	JETWEL
EASEL	SUW
SEÝÝÄS	SUWLAR

61 - Science Fiction

```
F W P G Z J V C G H T A I R
P Q R F R O G Z Ö M V K P O
S F G A H E R P R R Y I Ý B
E A Ý I G O L O N H E T A O
Q J C I N N O N Ü B Z K N T
H N P U T I T R Ş U I A G L
K I Z R D K Q A A D I L Y A
E L M S K Z Q M H C J A N R
J J O I S Y R L Y R L G G B
L K T N K Q G X R N I E V W
E T A I L A I P O T S Y D C
G A T E N A L P N V T G O Q
S R A E W G R A Ý I P O T U
K I T A P L A R R H X M D T
```

ATOM
KITAPLAR
HIMIKALAR
KINO
KLONLAR
DYSTOPI .A
EWG
ÝANGYN
GELJEK

GALAKTIKA
GÖRNÜŞ
SYRLY
ORACLE
PLANETA
ROBOTLAR
TEHNOLOGIÝA
UTOPIÝA

62 - Geometry

```
M N B A Q M P U S J I Q R T
C A H O T G B A W S S N A E
D I S I Ý R Q T R Z V F S O
T D L S K I S A A A X P A R
W E B N A L O G I K L M N I
A M F V X L K Q I S E L Y Ý
G U R A M A Y T Y D Ö G E A
H A S A P L A M A S S Ö B L
G O R I Z O N T A L Ü W Ö D
S Y M M E T R I D W Ş R L A
K L Q W E G R I Ä A U Ü Ü Ş
Q T Ö L Ç E G X B Q V M M K
I Ş L I K L E R I V N K U Y
Ü Ç Ü N J I Z J Ň X I X Z K
```

IŞLIKLER	MASSALY
HASAPLAMA	MEDIAN
DÄBIŇ	SANY
EGRI	PARALLEL
GÖWRÜM	ÖSÜŞ
ÖLÇEG	BÖLÜM
GURAMA	DAŞKY
BOÝ	SYMMETRI
GORIZONTAL	TEORIÝA
LOGIK	ÜÇÜNJI

63 - Creativity

```
I  G  Ö  R  Ü  Ş  L  E  R  C  E  J  Z  S
E  N  W  I  T  A  L  I  Ý  Ş  Y  Q  R  G
K  Y  T  P  L  N  E  D  N  Ü  Z  Ö  Z  Ö
H  Q  K  U  K  U  H  O  M  N  D  Z  W  P
N  A  L  K  I  T  A  M  A  R  D  T  X  A
N  V  V  T  E  S  D  E  H  Ö  Z  N  Q  T
A  E  A  A  E  H  I  G  L  G  O  E  P  L
G  X  Y  G  U  R  O  Ý  Y  Ş  R  A  G  Q
I  W  L  N  A  S  J  T  A  R  U  S  C  W
X  D  O  U  C  A  Ý  I  S  A  S  N  E  S
R  R  E  S  P  P  Z  N  M  F  Ö  W  H  Y
H  O  P  A  G  G  Ü  Ý  Ç  E  U  X  D  E
J  Y  B  P  S  V  R  A  L  U  G  Ý  U  D
Ö  W  R  E  N  M  E  K  K  A  I  E  X  I
```

SUNGAT	YLHAM
HUKUK	GÜÝÇ
GARŞY	INTUISIÝA
DRAMATIK	TERJIME
DUÝGULAR	SENSASIÝA
SÖUGI	ÖWRENMEK
IDEAS	ÖZ-ÖZÜNDEN
SURAT	GÖRÜŞLER
GÖRNÜŞ	WITALIÝ

64 - Airplanes

```
H A P G Ý O L A G Ç Y M B F
Y K N F U Q N W S Q Y I E U
R Q X D P R O C H B Y G L E
A Y U R E L L E P O R P E L
T D W G G R B U A B B B N Y
O M V N A M S A Ș T S M T K
K E U E E R H K I Y V L L P
A K J G N O L A B P K A I I
A I K O Y T P X Q B O Ý K L
I P P R A O U E O Z J Y H O
R A R D Z M R R Q H I G D T
Y Ž D I I H W A E C G Q P O
C P K G D D E S E N T F C H
A T M O S F E R A Y P T O X
```

ADVENTURE	FUEL
AIR	BOÝ
BELENTLIK	TARYH
ATMOSFERA	GIDROGEN
BALON	ANDER
GURLUȘYK	ÝOLAGÇY
EKIPAŽ	PILOT
DESENT	PROPELLER
DIZAYN	ASMAN
MOTOR	

65 - Ocean

```
K E P M E K Y L A B A R K W
O O Y R E G N Ü S E V A W M
Y T R M L F I T U N A N Y C
F U R A M M F V Y M P I M W
V M Ş Ý L I L N P D Z L H W
A L A A A S E D I T F A E Q
A H L P R D D T G E L B Y E
G D N C H K M F W K O Z E B
H R S Z Q V L A V B V K P A
U A L I T U P A N A I W H L
J L A Ň S A D X Q R T G Q Y
A G R E Ý F U O Y S T E R K
Z A U D Z Z Z R Q X W T T I
T U R T L A F S T Z S I M G
```

ALGA	DEŇIZ
KORAL	ŞARK
KRAB	BALYKEMP
DELFIN	SÜNGER
EEL	TUPAN
BALYK	TIDES
OTRÝAD	TUNA
OYSTER	TURTLA
REÝF	WAVES
DUZ	BALINA

66 - Force and Gravity

```
O B P G H Ç O R B I T E D M
R L Y A H Ä E Q X J U L D E
L B A I G M S K Q A G Y U R
H A M K B U J I I M N G N K
U T Z P Ş T H Z Ý Ş Y Ç A E
N G I Ň E L D I Ş E M I Z Z
I A T Q A R A L Y K T E R B
V G E T B A S Y Ş N G L Q W
E R N I F C A K I N A X E M
R A G Z U P K Y F H W B E R
S M A T Ä S I R L I L I K I
A Q M O L D Z V F T O W O N
L Y N S Y T I K S N J Q E D
J E U U H D F Q Z J Z Q D H
```

AKŞ	MEXANIKA
MERKEZ	ORBIT
AÇYŞ	FIZIKA
ARALYK	BASYŞ
IND	HÄSIÝETLER
GIŇELDIŞ	TIZ
ÇEKIŞME	WAGT
TÄSIRLILIK	UNIVERSAL
MAGNETIZM	AGRAM

67 - Birds

```
F  N  K  E  D  R  Ö  W  H  Q  X  X  I  P
L  L  E  A  T  Ü  G  R  Ü  B  F  V  J  E
A  Z  J  A  N  B  O  Q  L  F  I  C  H  L
M  D  Ç  K  S  A  Ý  N  Q  P  W  K  Q  I
I  I  A  I  R  V  R  O  S  T  R  I  H  K
N  R  U  M  K  K  A  Y  D  Q  K  W  U  A
G  Z  F  R  O  I  B  Q  O  Q  A  N  K  N
O  X  Y  N  C  I  A  M  W  O  R  K  K  H
P  A  R  R  O  T  H  N  E  U  G  N  E  P
S  W  A  N  B  R  Ç  X  L  D  P  C  K  V
F  B  G  X  E  X  E  S  E  R  Ç  E  W  W
C  V  V  K  W  M  P  G  G  H  D  Q  O  N
Ý  U  M  U  R  T  G  A  J  Q  U  V  Ý  P
T  O  U  K  A  N  U  X  E  Y  F  S  L  Z
```

KANARY	GERON
ÇIK	OSTRIH
KROW	PARROT
KEKWOÝ	PEÇ
DOWEL	PELIKAN
ÖRDEK	PENGUEN
BÜRGÜT	SERÇE
ÝUMURTGA	HABAR
FLAMINGO	SWAN
GOÝ	TOUKAN

68 - Nutrition

```
I  Ý  I  L  Ý  Ä  N  Ý  E  R  M  V  G  W
N  C  A  N  J  N  C  L  N  A  J  T  Ö  I
R  D  I  M  A  B  R  A  K  A  B  O  R  T
T  A  G  A  M  B  E  A  G  R  A  M  N  A
V  S  U  W  U  K  L  Y  K  L  A  R  Ü  M
V  J  O  X  L  V  T  I  M  Ý  I  C  Ş  I
B  L  P  N  C  Ş  I  R  I  D  Ň  I  S  N
S  A  G  L  Y  K  B  S  Ç  Ý  S  L  Q  B
Y  I  S  J  J  G  A  R  O  G  F  L  Y  E
B  Q  L  B  A  P  H  Ý  W  P  R  L  K  R
A  Ý  I  S  A  T  N  E  M  R  E  F  F  H
L  K  A  L  O  R  I  Ý  A  L  A  R  O  I
A  N  S  Z  A  G  F  N  H  K  M  O  W  Z
N  I  S  K  O  T  E  Ý  I  S  Ä  H  H  K
```

GÖRNÜŞ	HABITLER
BALAN	SAGLYK
AJY	SUWUKLYKLAR
KALORIÝALAR	IÝMIT
KARBAMID	GORAG
BERHIZ	HÄSIÝET
SIŇDIRIŞ	SÇÝS
IÝILÝÄN ÝER	TOKSIN
FERMENTASIÝA	WITAMIN
TAGAM	AGRAM

69 - Hiking

```
K H T H U D C S R G Ý G G A
Y A A W O H C U X V A Ü O Ý
L T M Ý N D Y W O G D N L A
R R I P W L F F T A A E L K
A A L B I A V F I R W V A G
Ý K K S A N N I M A S L N A
Ý D H C O Q G L M L Q S M P
A S R W C D Z K A K O Q A Z
T T E B I G A T S R K R L C
A E C Y I E B P R A L Ş A D
Ş B W U P V Q C N P Q N R Q
Ý T G C H N D K Q R E W Y O
A H U H N Z R Ü P G F I D H
G J V V C X F R Ş U O Z U J
```

HAÝWANLAR
AÝAKGAP
KAMPING
KLIFF
KLIMAT
GOLLANMALAR
GOWY
KARTA
DÜŞ
TEBIGAT

GAÝŞAT
PARKLAR
TAÝÝARLYK
DAŞLAR
SAMMIT
GÜN
ÝADAW
SUW
HOWA

70 - Professions #1

```
P P G E I Ş Z O E C I A M J
S P L O K N A B Q S C T N Z
I R Y U L A T Ý L S X J Z W
H O D F M C I T S I N A Ý P
O Y B N I B U C Q E C N L M
L Y A W Ç Y E U Q L P V P O
O F A R G O T R A K M L I N
G H G E O L O G T B E U E O
Ş E P A G A T U Ý A S Y G R
D E Ň I Z Ç I Ç L I N V T T
H L R K O M E N D I Ý A R S
S Z T A Ň K E D I T Ç I O A
D O K T O R O R U K O R P E
Z W T A N S Ç Y T Q S T U B
```

ILÇI	AWÇY
ASTRONOM	ŞAÝ-SEPLER
PROKUROR	MUGT
BANK	ŞEPAGAT UÝASY
KARTOGRAF	PÝANISTI
KOMENDIÝA	PLUMBER
TANSÇY	PSIHOLOG
DOKTOR	DEŇIZÇI
EDITÇI	TAŇK
GEOLOG	

71 - Barbecues

```
L O U M N A C S X Ç O P F G
V T L U M L R N N A Ý O I Ö
W Z Y S S Y N F M G U M L R
V E W I M J O E V A N I D N
S G Q K P R W W Q L L D U Ü
G O M A Ş G A L A A A O Z Ş
N N G S T O R Y L R R R F L
H Q T A A O Ç I K G A L O E
V F I O N L M C D N L A R R
C H M K A H A U B Y T R K Y
P Y Ý E Z C M D S X S Z L P
G R I L L R X I L U O E A N
A Ç L Y K S Ç Ý S A D C R J
B I L E N L E R V E R Z C F
```

ÇIK	AÇLYK
ÇAGALAR	BILENLER
MAŞGALA	MUSIK
IÝMIT	SOGAN
FORKLAR	SALADLAR
DOSTLAR	DUZ
MIWE	SÇÝS
OÝUNLAR	TOMUS
GRILL	POMIDORLAR
YSSY	GÖRNÜŞLER

72 - Chocolate

```
K A R A M E L S S W H T K A
K A L O R I Ý A L A R A O N
I N G R E D I E N T N G K T
Ş E K E R T A G A M F A O I
A H E B X H G X O D Z M N O
X B F K W Q W Z R Y V L U K
J M N L Z V S O R P F Y T S
N J S A I O C U A J Y B V I
E W S G J X T R F K I Q W D
H A L A Ý A N I N O A J L A
B Q Ç Ý Ü G Z I K Q E K S N
E F M U S H Ä S I Ý E T F T
G R E S E P T A G N U S D H
P E Ý D A L Y G X E H C G H
```

ANTIOKSIDANT
SUNGAT
AJY
KAKAO
KALORIÝALAR
KARAMEL
KOKONUT
TAGAMLY
EKZOTIK

HALAÝAN
INGREDIENT
PEÝDALY
GÜÝÇ
HÄSIÝET
RESEPT
ŞEKER
SÜÝJI
TAGAM

73 - Vegetables

```
A G P B F K S P G L E P K P
H A E R P Ö L E R V J L U O
J R Ý O O P T O L L A Ş L M
N L A K G E L E S E M X I I
M I D K U Ň R W Y Q R R F D
S K D O R R Y R W H E I L O
Ý A Y L K A D Ş U M G K O R
T Ü L I M D G W F U N A W N
U T P L N I K N I W I R E U
R R W E A Ş S K X T G O R K
N N S D K N S K O Ç I T R A
I C L Q S I D P A R S Y M V
P X G Z G F Y Y V Z U O D G
T J T Ü R K M E N I K Ş U P
```

ARTIÇOK	KÖPEŇ
BROKKOLI	PARSY
KAROT	PEÝA
KULIFLOWER	PUŞKIN
SELERI	RADIŞ
TÜRKMEN	SALLANDY
MESELE	ŞALLOT
GARLIK	ÝÜPEKI
GINGER	POMIDOR
MUŞDAK	TURNIP

74 - Boats

```
P V F G Ä M I M D Q V G N M
U B U G N M X A E R K X E L
K C T A Z N Q L Ň A A H Ý U
A W E R I Ý A X I L Ý F I S
J Z O Y R Q X W Z T A B T B
W B N K R I N D Ç G K K U H
K R A Y E L Ö G I K O U A Ý
B L K G F O K E A N D T N P
C U Q S D T Z R S V F Q M Ý
A T S K E K I P A Ž C L Y A
Q M U T L Q Ň O M O T O R H
G Ä M I S I E R Z J O H R T
V H B Y Z A D U R M U Ş B X
W I Y Z A K M T G Y C X C B
```

GÄMI   MAST
BUÝ   NAUTIÝEN
KANOE   OKEAN
EKIPAŽ   RAFT
DOK   AWERIÝA
MOTOR   ROP
FERRI   GÄMISI
KAÝAK   DEŇIZÇI
GÖLE   DEŇIZ
DURMUŞ   ÝAHT

75 - Activities and Leisure

```
B  J  Y  L  O  B  Ý  E  L  O  W  R  R  B
T  A  H  A  Ý  Y  S  B  O  K  S  B  A  A
R  E  L  I  B  O  H  X  B  B  I  P  A  G
A  H  O  Y  K  N  C  R  Z  G  N  B  I  B
P  U  B  H  K  L  A  O  Ý  N  N  Q  V  A
J  T  T  K  C  Ç  A  P  E  I  E  M  R  N
N  L  E  G  I  I  Y  F  B  P  T  A  A  Ç
X  Y  K  Y  Ö  E  U  L  N  M  U  D  T  Y
J  V  S  Q  F  R  F  O  Y  A  F  K  M  L
I  J  A  M  B  Q  N  G  K  K  A  Y  A  Y
L  O  B  T  U  F  G  Ü  O  Y  R  N  K  K
D  Ü  K  A  N  D  N  L  Ş  C  T  G  K  N
U  A  S  U  R  F  I  N  G  K  V  B  W  D
S  U  W  D  A  Ý  Ü  Z  M  E  K  S  C  A
```

ART	HOBILER
BEÝZBOL	GÖRNÜŞ
BASKETBOL	DÜKAN
BOKS	FUTBOL
KAMPING	SURFING
AIVRATMAK	SUWDA ÝÜZMEK
BALYKÇYLYK	TENNIS
BAGBANÇYLYK	SYÝAHAT
GOLF	WOLEÝBOL

76 - Driving

```
G T P O L I S I Ý A K P V X
N I X P E B C H F T I Y F G
G Z S L N G H X T R L Ý L N
M I F X U B P E X A I A H A
Y B F S T G N P R K Ç D F Y
E E W A O W P U T Z K A D V
F U E L R W U W V A Ä P S X
G I I M O T O S I K L O O F
C V J G T K D Q A M E I A R
H A Ü J O M S Z Z H H Q B E
O B R E M U C G A R A J Y N
W Ş Ü N R Ö G W B G A S Y L
P W S H O W P S U Z L Y K E
V U L I S E N Z I Ý A K L R
```

HELÄKÇILIK	MOTOR
FRENLER	MOTOSIKL
CAR	PYÝADA
HOWP	POLISIÝA
SÜRÜJI	OOL
FUEL	HOWPSUZLYK
GARAJY	TIZ
GAZ	TRAFIG
LISENZIÝA	GÖRNÜŞ
KARTA	TUNEL

77 - Professions #2

```
D I V Ž Z O O L O G F C W K
D F N X U B A G Ş Y T F K I
P I C W L R E M R E F R A T
X I L S E N N F I Z I K I A
L A L H U N D A X R I X G P
C D M O D R T L L Q Y Ş Ö H
F D O Z T Y W O A I T E Z A
M U G A L L Y M R I S K L N
F I L O S O F X J N I T E A
F O T O G R A F N Ž W A G M
A S T R O N A W T E G R Ç H
D E G I Ş M Ä X L N N U I S
B I O L O G V S U E I S T Y
H I R U R G K K J R L S F Q
```

ASTRONAWT
BIOLOG
DEGIŞMÄ
INŽENER
FERMER
BAGŞY
INWENTOR
ŽURNALIST
KITAPHANA
LINGWIST

SURATKEŞ
FILOSOF
FOTOGRAF
FIZIKI
PILOT
GÖZLEGÇI
HIRURG
MUGALLYM
ZOOLOG

78 - Mythology

```
A R H E T I P G G A R A Ş Y
M W S B U E K X Ü C L G X J
C P N O Z A L E C Ý R Ş V R
Ö L Ü M O R E G D T Ç Y Y C
Y J L Q N Y S Ö G I R D C T
E N R A P Z E W Ö B Y A B V
R A A C T D K I L P I R Ö G
T Ž L N G Ö K Y Ş Y K A Z B
E D R M M F X H H N W E U R
K A Ň V H A V K O P R R V E
I R A I Z O K I L M Ü H Ö M
L H T D Ö R E D I J I L I K
E A M E D E N I Ý E T I W E
R L A B I R I N T N V W Z L
```

ARHETIP	MÖHÜMLIK
SÖ .GI	GÖRIPLIK
YNANMAK	LABIRINT
REARADYŞ	ERTEKILER
DÖREDIJILIK	YŞYK
MEDENIÝET	AŽDARHA
TAŇRLAR	ÖLÜM
KESEL	ÖWEZ
GÖK	GÜÝÇ
GERO	GARAŞY

79 - Hair Types

```
G S K Y R U G B W D B Ş E C
I F S E A G S Y G G Ö I H T
S J A D L A B G C A R N C N
E J G E D L J K A R Ü A T C
U Y L B I G E Y Q A P Ý S U
Ç B Y E A G O L B Ş Ü M Ü K
R Y K S R A G K E I N Ç E I
X Q K L B S Z A V R J P S Y
X D C E D U Q Ş F O X N E D
X Y R F H A W M R U Z A K J
R E Ň K L I A U P I K I R W
K Ö R E Ç E W Ý N P R J I A
L I V R L X W L V W T G U U
W Z O D V M A E E N I G E H
```

BALD	SAGLYK
GAR	UZAK
BÖRÜP	ŞINAÝ
BRAIDLAR	GYSGA
GARAŞ	KÜMÜŞ
REŇKLI	ÝUMŞAKLYK
KELLELER	PIKIR
KÖREÇE	INÇE
GURY ..	WAWWA
ÇYK	AK

80 - Furniture

```
J F C G A P G A Ç L A R R Z
P E G I N E Ş I K G M F O U
U S G D L X A L H Z R R H H
B E N Ç U O K A M G F L I A
P P I H G Y S G A Ç A V M M
C P C W L K Y M G H A J H M
I X Y S F A B P S F N Ý G O
O D T C A C E I E S U K N K
F R I A H C D L D N G T O A
M A T R E S S L K T Z K O U
N N G Y P U C O Q Y V N C N
R I A Ç M R A W B Y Z E D L
A Ý K E S E L L E R S H H U
F T G I O C L K K I T A P M
```

ARMÇAIR	EGIN-EŞIK
BED	FUTON
BENÇ	HAMMOK
KITAP	ÇYRA
CHAIR	MATRESS
KOUÇ	AÝNA
GYSGAÇA	PILLOW
KESELLER	RÝG
DESGA	GAP-GAÇLAR

81 - Garden

```
G  S  R  Y  S  R  O  R  Ç  A  R  D  G  T
I  V  P  Y  J  A  R  A  G  S  I  B  G  H
C  B  E  N  Ç  K  F  L  A  Ý  Y  W  Y  H
I  K  H  I  Ş  E  H  T  B  A  K  K  U  A
V  J  D  L  O  U  X  O  C  K  G  K  M  M
Z  H  K  O  W  U  B  N  C  J  L  A  W  M
T  A  L  P  E  Z  O  B  G  Q  N  Ş  Ç  O
E  Ş  S  M  L  H  O  W  D  A  N  R  U  K
R  A  J  A  L  V  L  N  J  Q  K  O  Q  A
A  L  P  R  V  Z  D  P  G  Ü  L  P  X  R
S  Ý  Ü  T  H  W  R  K  W  S  X  U  D  P
U  A  Q  Z  D  W  J  F  K  G  N  R  C  O
C  R  I  O  Ü  A  R  G  U  K  X  T  K  T
M  N  K  H  D  M  A  B  V  R  J  R  V  G
```

BENÇ	HOWDAN
BUŞ	PORŞAK
KAÝS	RAKE
GÜL	ŞOWEL
GARAJY	TOPRAK
BAG	TERAS
OTLAR	TRAMPOLIN
HAMMOK	AGAÇ
HOZ	ÜZÜM
ORÇARD	HAŞALÝAR

82 - Diplomacy

```
J E M G Y Ý E T A L A D A A
D I P L O M A T I K O Z D Ý
H Ç Ç Y R A Ý A T L A R A Y
I L Ö Q N Y G O T Y O B Ş P
H I Z A V S S E E T I M A S
O L Ü M N N A E M H P T R Y
W Ç W N M A N N Ü Ç F X Y Z
P I E W X K W L K Ö H U Ý L
S H R J F K C R Ö Z U A U Y
U A A J M Z Y D H G X H R K
Z N Ý Q E W U P J Ü I E T K
L A A K F D U K I T I L O P
Y B T Y T D E T E R J I M E
K Y Ç T A H A L S A M U Y Y
```

MASLAHATÇY	HÖKÜMET
ILÇI	YNSAN
RAÝATLAR	AÝYPSYZLYK
RAÝAT	ADALAT
JEMGYÝET	POLITIK
DIPLOMATIK	ÇÖZGÜT
JEDEL	HOWPSUZLYK
ILÇIHANA	ÇÖZÜW
ETIM	TERJIME
DAŞARY ÝURT	

83 - Countries #1

```
W  M  Y  M  Ü  S  Ü  R  F  O  W  U  V  N
Ý  A  P  S  N  D  L  A  T  W  I  Ý  A  O
E  Ý  O  P  R  S  E  N  E  G  A  L  A  R
T  I  L  X  P  A  D  A  N  A  K  S  H  W
N  D  Ş  W  A  Y  Ý  F  M  Y  M  A  U  E
A  N  A  S  N  F  R  Y  Z  O  O  Ý  A  G
M  A  F  Q  A  E  C  A  L  I  R  I  Ý  I
L  L  P  G  M  E  J  U  K  R  O  L  I  Ý
I  N  A  D  A  U  G  A  R  A  K  I  N  A
B  I  S  P  A  N  I  Ý  A  Ý  K  Z  Y  W
I  F  W  V  Y  F  Y  D  V  L  O  A  M  A
Ý  N  S  Y  J  P  V  H  G  A  W  R  U  Y
A  L  E  U  Z  E  N  E  W  T  M  B  R  B
G  E  R  M  A  N  I  Ý  A  I  Q  O  U  W
```

BRAZILIÝA	MOROKKO
KANADA	NIKARAGUA
MÜSÜR	NORWEGIÝA
FINLANDIÝA	PANAMA
GERMANIÝA	POLŞA
YRAK	RUMYNIÝA
YSRAÝYL	SENEGAL
ITALÝA	ISPANIÝA
LATWIÝA	WENEZUELA
LIBIÝA	WÝETNAM

84 - Adjectives #1

```
A J R B E M Ö H Ü M W C V N
G R K Q Ç K E M Ö K O U B J
Ö V O O N W Z G A R A Ň K Y
Z O H M I X W O U M U M Y L
E J G L A Ý A H T B N E E U
L I M Ä K T F I Y I W O J T
B A G T L Y I V O V K B K C
W T F F G S T K N N R M F C
Q P I D D U K I H T G M U J
G O W Y L N A G R A S O C Y
G F K W C G M Z F C V R W C
Y V M A F A M C Y Z B E J Y
U V A O O T A B S O L Ý U T
H Ä Z I R K I Z A M A N L D
```

ABSOLÝUT	KÖMEK
AROMATIK	ION GOWY
SUNGAT	ULY
GÖZEL	MÖHÜM
GARAŇKY	HÄZIRKI ZAMAN
EKZOTIK	KÄMIL
UMUMY	AGRAS
BAGTLY	HAÝAL
GOWY	INÇE

85 - Technology

```
K O M P Ý U T E R Z W K P D
H G W I R T U A L V I D R V
A E N Q A Z X R G D R N O M
B L K L V R F E Ö B U M G A
A Z K R G U A M R K S A R K
R Ö M R A O Ý A N A L X A Y
F G M S I N L K Ü L P N M L
B Z W C P Z A B Ş A U P M Z
T T E N R E T N I M G E A U
F B G O A K I T S I T A T S
K U R S O R G J R B A Ý T P
J Y E K E J I X Y W O C T W
W U Z O H D D W P X V E B O
M A G L U M A T L A R C U H
```

BLOG   INTERNET
GÖRNÜŞ   HABAR
BAÝT   GÖZLEG
KAMERA   EKRAN
KOMPÝUTER   HOWPSUZLYK
KURSOR   PROGRAMMA
MAGLUMATLAR   STATISTIKA
DIGITAL   WIRTUAL
FAÝL   WIRUS
KALAM

86 - Landscapes

```
B H R U C R P X N S B B U P
L D M X Z C D B Z Ä M A M A
L X E Y O M F P Z W F T K R
G O W A K K S D W E L G Q N
A L U S N I N E P R W A A D
Ý D D F N L A L P P U L J Z
I K E P C L E Ö D A L Y A O
R C E Ň N Ä K G Ü K K K R X
E B E N I B O Q Ş L A V D P
W E W B A Z H S F A N S N R
A H W K E R U I B U Z L U K
S B R L T R E Z Ý E G Z T M
U O F R V J G A D A R H Ä S
W T G M A F X O B E J Q E L
```

KENAR	OAZIS
GOWAK	OKEAN
SÄHRA	PENINSULA
GEÝZER	AWERIÝA
BUZLUK	DEŇIZ
BÄLLIK	BATGALYK
ICEBERG	TUNDRA
ADA	SÄWER
GÖLE	WULKAN
DÜŞ	SUW

87 - Visual Arts

```
S U N G A T Ç Y K Z L P Z S
T R S D G Z O K E M V O F T
R Ä X A Q V K I R W Y N J E
M G T B K Y Ç L A P X I F N
J E G W C A G I M L I F J C
Q Z K R A P X J I P E S P I
I Ý V D Ş X K I K P L Y F L
T Ü M Z E Ü E D A G A L A M
T K M I W P N E Ç A L Y R Z
Q X B U T Ç A R K O A L G D
Ş A H S Y E T Ö Ö P N E O U
M I K F X I S D E G A S T K
N A R H I T E K T U R A O X
M A S T E R P I E C E E F G
```

ARHITEKTURA	MASTERPIECE
SUNGATÇY	GÖRNÜŞ
KERAMIKA	GALAM
ÇALY ..	ŞAHSY .ET
ÇARKOAL	FOTOGRAF
PALÇYK	KÜÝZEGÄR
DÖREDIJILIK	MEKDEP
EASEL	STENCIL
FILM	WAX

88 - Plants

```
W C N N O X P K X R F X L M
E H A K I N A T O B O T L E
G S Ý E D O E K S N L O H A
E T E N E Ç I R Y C I K G E
T I B B Z V A X P O Ý A J L
A Z X S T E M G A B A Ý U T
S L A S Q S U U A Ž K A J
I Q H O A X P O S M C Ö Y T
Ý H J M V R N B G B Z K W Y
A W L A U B O B H U I U Z R
Y U W A R U T P E K I V K M
P E T E K Ş L X U R O L Y G
V O Q S V O A X C H R K A Ü
K A K T U S R C W I C I A L
```

BAMBUK	BAG
BEÝAN	OTLAR
BERRI	IVY
BOTANIKA	MOSS
BUŞ	PETEK
KAKTUS	KÖK
TENEÇIR	STEM
GÜL	AGAÇ
FOLIÝAŽ	WEGETASIÝA
TOKAÝ	

89 - Countries #2

```
G S O M A L I Ý A C R Z U R
E A Ý I R E B I L D U F I K
F K I T F D P X V D S N I D
I I A T M A Z N D P S R I V
O A L Q I N N A T S I K Ä P
P M B S Y I A D O L Ý X H Z
I A A P I Ý D N M Y A S P O
Ý J N X F A U A T S Ý P P F
A Ý I R I S S G O K I H E M
L V Ý J B L V U R M R A N N
L I A Ý I N O P A Ý E E O N
A U W G R E S I Ý A G P D M
O S T A N I A R K U I B Y J
S U F Y N C Z Y B T N T K D
```

ALBANIÝA
DANIÝA
EFIOPIÝA
GRESIÝA
GAITI
JAMAIKA
ÝAPONIÝA
LAOS
LIWAN
LIBERIÝA

MEHIKO
NEPAL
NIGERIÝA
PÄKISTAN
RUSSIÝA
SOMALIÝA
SUDAN
SIRIÝA
UGANDA
UKRAINA

90 - Adjectives #2

```
E Z T S O W G A T B L D O G
A Z Q E Z Ä T A T B O M S Ü
I U D B B K Y L Y N A B A Ý
A K I L R I B P E K E T L Ç
G Ç O E I B G M G O S V T L
Y E L G T Y K Y K A H A Y I
Z N K Y H V A R E L M Ü N Ö
Y U T L K V R U H Ş E M V E
K Y Z V Z D U G L H W C L O
L S U A N Y A S A G L Y K W
Y S G O K H Z N M M H R W A
R Y E Y Q Ý A R A D Y J Y D
J O G A P K Ä R Ç I L I K A
D Ü Ş Ü N D I R I Ş A H A N
```

HAKYKY	GYZYKLY
ÝARADYJY	TEBIGY
DÜŞÜNDIRIŞ	TÄZE
GURY ..	ÖNÜMLER
OWADAN	TEKEPBIRLIK
MEŞHUR	JOGAPKÄRÇILIK
SOWGAT	SALTY
SAGLYK	UZAK
YSSY	GÜÝÇLI
AÇLYKDAN	ÝABANYLYK

91 - Math

```
P G G S G X P G I G M U Ö S
A E H Y Y B O U R Ö V E L L
R O I M S K L R H R F P A H
A M K M G I I O M N N E R S
L E I E A L G L W Ü R R I A
L T N T Ç I O T N Ş J I T N
E R J R A Ç N I M O N M M L
L I I I E E B U K D Y E E A
O Ý A D Y M Ü R W Ö G T T R
G A F M V I J N Ü Ç Ü R I Q
R L Y K A J I Z V B M I K Y
A O R P A R A L L E L O H Q
M C V I R E U K M Q M P W S
X R E Z X T U G I M E I D M
```

BUKDY
ARITMETIK
TERJIMEÇILIK
ONLIK
GÖWRÜM
GURAMA
GYSGAÇA
GEOMETRIÝA
SANLAR

PARALLEL
PARALLELOGRAM
PERIMETRI
POLIGON
GÖRNÜŞ
IKINJI
SYMMETRI
ÜÇÜNJI
SÖUMGI

92 - Water

```
S G F I R O K E A N Y C T S
W N G P A I E K C R N L O H
X F O V I U M A Y I S E L O
S V I W N B Ç L Y G A U K W
R I V E R O İ L Q D N G U E
T A S R J T O F U O L E N R
B Z O U L L V S L Ö Y Y L E
M A E T S W A N N S K S A X
F Ý T S V N M J C O I E R D
N A K I R R U G U N M R X Y
U W L O G S F T Z P G N A J
O K A M A L G U B K A N A L
B L Y R J P T V S R A Q W V
S U W A R Y Ş T R I P U O G
```

KANAL	LAKE
IÇMEK	MOISTURE
BUGLAMAK	MONSOON
SÖODGI	OKEAN
AÝAZ	RAIN
GEYSER	RIVER
YNSANLYK	SHOWER
GURRIKAN	SNOW
ICE	STEAM
SUWARYŞ	TOLKUNLAR

93 - Activities

```
F  H  K  A  M  P  I  N  G  W  B  N  C  P
O  Y  Q  O  G  A  D  Y  Ş  R  A  G  J  S
T  Z  W  Y  I  D  X  Y  Ş  Z  G  E  T  U
O  M  A  Z  A  T  O  Y  Y  K  B  V  E  D
S  A  M  E  D  Q  I  K  L  I  A  O  M  B
U  T  N  I  K  I  T  R  A  L  N  U  Ý  O
R  L  A  T  P  B  G  P  Ç  Ý  Ç  A  D  B
A  A  L  P  A  T  Z  V  N  Ö  Y  W  E  W
T  R  K  F  Y  N  S  C  Y  G  L  I  C  A
Q  Ş  Y  Ý  A  H  S  C  D  Y  Y  Ş  N  R
P  R  Z  H  F  R  T  O  R  D  K  L  I  T
J  K  Y  L  Y  Ç  K  Y  L  A  B  E  T  R
K  H  G  H  N  L  K  G  C  J  G  R  X  W
U  G  E  P  U  Z  Z  L  E  M  E  L  E  R
```

IŞLER	GYZYKLANMA
ART	DYNÇ ALYŞ
KAMPING	JADYGÖÝLIK
HYZMATLAR	FOTOSURAT
TANS	HAÝYŞ
BALYKÇYLYK	PUZZLEMELER
OÝUNLAR	OKA
BAGBANÇYLYK	GARŞY
AW	TIKIN

94 - Business

```
K  I  Ş  L  E  R  E  J  E  N  E  M  S  A
M  A  I  U  E  X  P  G  V  Q  L  Y  A  Y
A  Ý  R  P  Y  I  V  Q  Y  I  C  Y  T  Z
Ý  I  I  I  Q  I  I  C  U  S  R  X  L  A
A  N  G  E  Ý  I  L  A  M  I  G  L  Y  W
G  A  D  G  G  E  X  R  L  F  T  A  K  O
O  P  G  Ü  S  O  R  S  K  O  K  K  Ç  D
Ý  M  E  J  K  L  V  A  O  U  B  P  R  A
U  O  Ç  G  R  A  L  T  Y  G  L  A  S  Z
M  K  I  F  O  K  N  G  I  R  D  E  J  I
M  P  Ş  B  Ý  U  J  E  T  Z  H  J  L  E
K  C  C  T  L  X  H  H  A  R  Y  T  X  C
A  R  Z  A  N  L  A  M  A  G  N  J  F  D
Y  K  D  Y  S  A  D  Y  Ý  E  T  U  X  R
```

BÝUJET
KARIÝERA
KOMPANIÝA
HARYT
GYSGAÇA
ARZANLAMA
YKDYSADYÝET
IŞLER
ZAWOD
MALIÝE

GIRIŞ
MAÝA GOÝUM
MENEJER
PUL
OFIS
GIRDEJI
SATLYK
DÜKAN
SALGYTLAR
GEÇIŞ

95 - Literature

```
T R A D I Ý A Y W I V Y O I
F L P K S D E P Ş Z Y G A Y
B I O G R A F I Ý A T E M A
A N T Z P R Y H A Ş B W F V
C W P F L O U B A G R Ý W P
P A T S N F A Ç G Y T E A T
O N G O L A I D C N D A Ý N
E A I H R T A N E K D O T M
M L J K R E P E Ç K Y E C R
A I Y P J M I Ş L I K L E R
M Z D E Ň E Ş D I R M E Y D
R O W R S T O S L A M A R A
A A N A L O G I Ý A Z X Y T
D N E T I J E S K C L D M S
```

ANALOGIÝA	METAFORA
ANALIZ	NAÝBAŞY
ANEKDOT	ÇEPER
AWTOR	POEMA
BIOGRAFIÝA	ŞAHYR
DEŇEŞDIRME	REÝM
NETIJE	YRYM
AÇGYT	IŞLIKLER
DIALOG	TEMA
TOSLAMA	TRADIÝA

96 - Geography

```
G R J H O M I I U F O Y S K
E Ü E D U T I T A L W F N K
Y X N G D C J Y O D K J O P
O O K O I V Y S D Ü Ş K Z S
K U A T R O K A W E R I Ý A
E U R U E T N R A F U F Y L
A R T T H S A M C D H J Z T
N T A Y Ä E T E O V A N X A
L Y D J Ş W O H D E Ň I Z I
B E L E N T L I K D Ü N L D
W M E R I D I Ý A N C L A G
K O N T I N E N T H X K P L
D E M I R G A Z Y K O X E I
T E R R I T O R I Ý A U G I
```

BELENTLIK
ATLAS
ŞÄHER
KONTINENT
OUURT
HEMRASY
ADA
LATITUDE
KARTA
MERIDIÝAN

DÜŞ
DEMIRGAZYK
OKEAN
REGION
AWERIÝA
DEŇIZ
GÜNORTA
TERRITORIÝA
WEST
DÜNLD

97 - Pets

```
H G K S C G P S A R K M V H
Ş Ý E L G B E H B B S U C K
K E P Ö K O W Ç I Ý M I T R
K Y D L P M Q K I L U P C D
O R E L E R I J N E P R G P
T H R A N I R E T E W G U I
U A I G N Q D T O W Ş A N Ş
L I Z A R D G T E H E U D I
P G S Ç A B V A L T R U T K
A U U T L V A M M K E F Q P
R Ý W M L X R L S S S Z U Q
R R M A O E K P Y A T Z C F
O U Z N K W R S E K H E X Y
T K S Y Ç A N J Y K G F R G
```

PIŞIK	LEÝŞ
PENJIRELER	LIZARD
KOLLAR	SYÇANJYK
KOW	PARROT
KÖPEK	ÇAGA
BALYK	TOWŞAN
IÝMIT	GUÝRUK
GEÇI	TURTLA
GAMSTER	WETERINAR
KEPDERI	SUW

98 - Jazz

```
A T F C T G A J T Ä Z E Q C
A Ý I S I Z O P M O K L M J
D L D W T S T W U E M R M G
N H M Y R Y H A Z W L Y A U
X T C D M Ş N Y G T A P S M
D V B M J Q Y T R M O B L A
X E M U S I K K E N F D A D
S U N G A T N A L A T R H Ü
H X J Ö X B Q T K A R U A Z
M D T A K Q J B I T E M T G
M E Ş H U R R Q L J S L L Ü
O R K E S T R E Ş J N A A N
T E H N I K A T I V O R R J
K O M P O Z I T O R K N F V
```

ALBOM	DÜZGÜN
ALKYŞ	MUSIK
SUNGAT	TÄZE
KOMPOZITOR	KÖNE
KOMPOZISIÝA	ORKESTR
KONSERT	YRYM
DRUMLAR	AÝDYM
NYGTAP	IŞLIKLER
MEŞHUR	TALANT
MASLAHATLAR	TEHNIKA

99 - Nature

```
B U Z L U K I L L E Z Ö G H
Y Y R A U T K N A S J X W A
A F I P R K I F P E Q Q Z Ý
R R O Q D H P M L T F O G W
H A K L N X O E H W V Z P A
Ä L E T I C R E T L E Ş A N
S Z R A I Ý T E M S F C R L
H Y O U R K A T O K A Ý A A
O G Z P U Y R Ž S B Z E H R
O T I A D Y L Y Z D R U A I
G G Ý K L I E A P R A V T O
Q G A M Ö H Ü M R U N G L A
N P U Z S E R P A Ý I V Y Y
A W E R I Ý A V S R I Y K O
```

HAÝWANLAR	TOKAÝ
ARKTIK	BUZLUK
GÖZELLIK	PARAHATLYK
ARYLAR	AWERIÝA
GYZLAR	SANKTUARY
SÄHRA	SERPAÝ
IND	ŞELTER
EROZIÝA	TROPIKI
FOG	MÖHÜM
FOLIÝAŽ	

100 - Vacation #2

```
H E D G U A D A Ş A M A K F
D O K A V T V I S A I I G N
Y M W O Ş R D M J G T L Q J
N Y B A P A D Q R Y Z E R R
Ç H H D M K R A L T A R U S
A M B A Q E G Y D A S K A M
L A V O U Ş N D Ý Ç A D Y R
Y N P U N I I Z S U Z Z F C
Ş H A L E M P L I H R I O U
M A S G P L M N S L V T H G
T N P H D E A J K C I Ý O L
C A O X W G K O A D E Ň I Z
F O R A N E K R T O V W Y N
R Z T R E S T O R A N J C I
```

HOWA MENZILI	KARTA
KENAR	PASPORT
KAMPING	SURATLAR
MAKSADY	RESTORAN
DAŞARY ÝURT	DEŇIZ
GELMIŞEK	TAKSI
MYHMANHANA	ÇADYR
ADA	DAŞAMAK
ÝOL	VISA
DYNÇ ALYŞ	

1 - Antiques

2 - Food #1

3 - Measurements

4 - Farm #2

5 - Books

6 - Meditation

7 - Days and Months

8 - Energy

9 - Archeology

10 - Food #2

11 - Chemistry

12 - Music

13 - Family

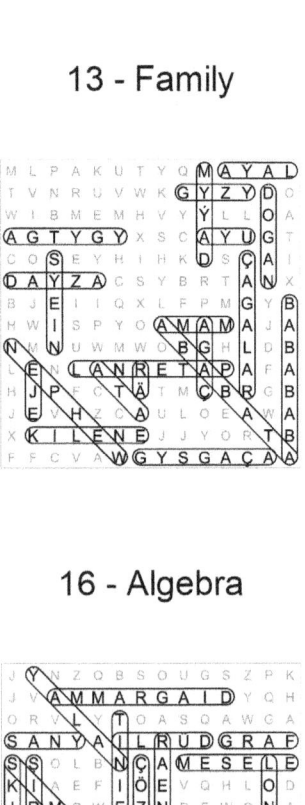

14 - Farm #1

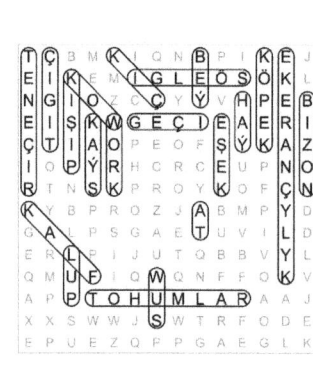

15 - Camping

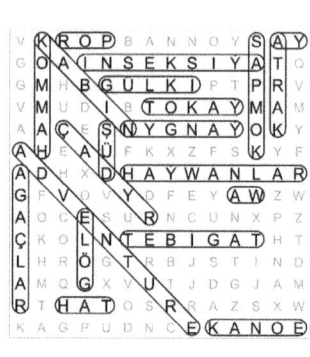

16 - Algebra

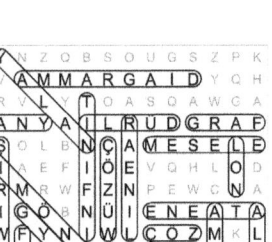
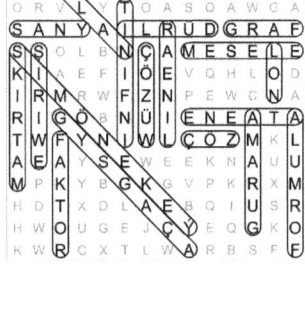

17 - Numbers

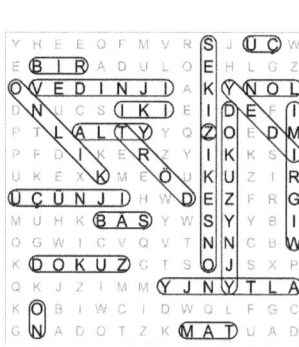
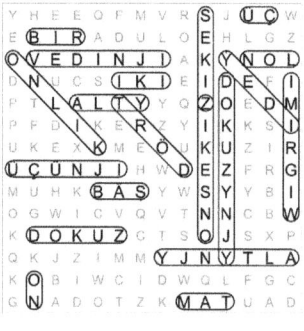

18 - Spices

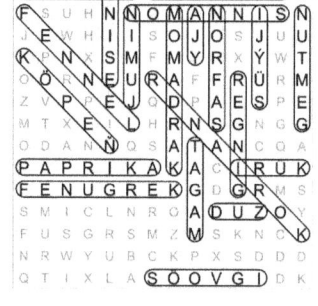

19 - Universe

20 - Mammals

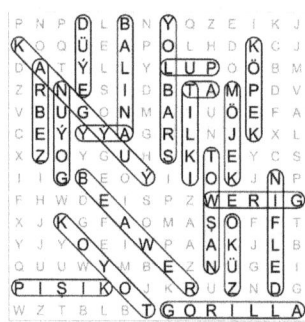

21 - Fishing

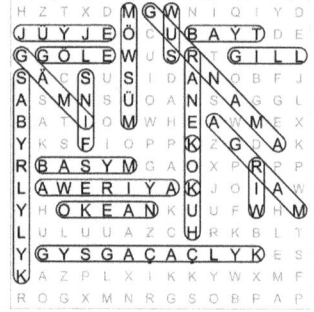

22 - Bees

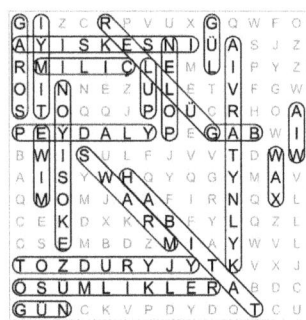

23 - Photography

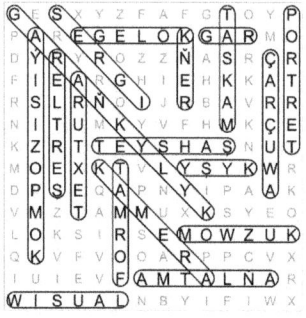

24 - Weather

25 - Adventure

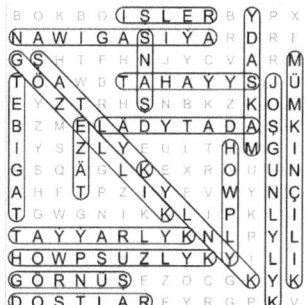

26 - Sport

27 - Circus

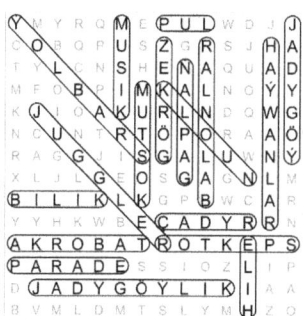

28 - Geology

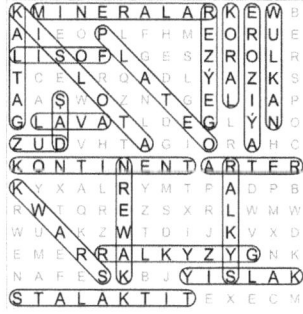

29 - House

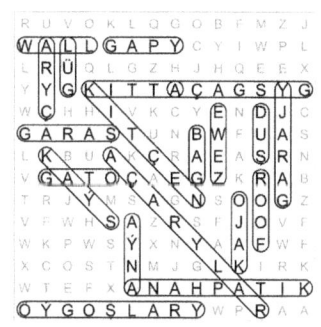

30 - Physics

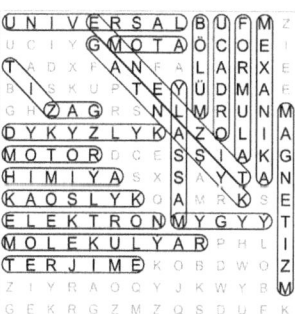

31 - Dance

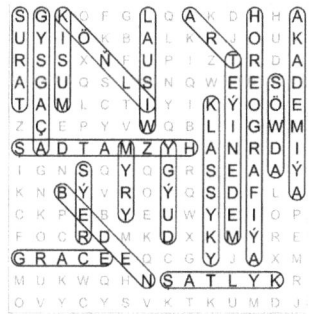

32 - Colors

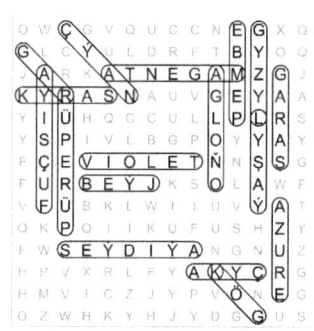

33 - Shapes

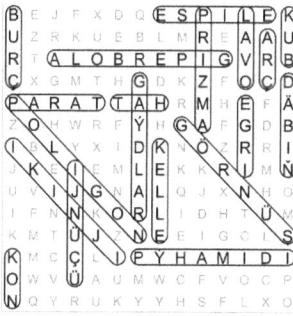

34 - Scientific Disciplines

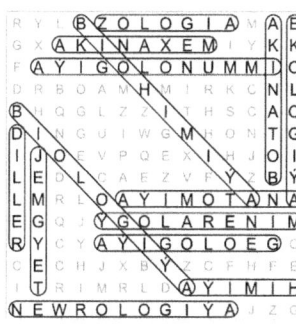

35 - Science

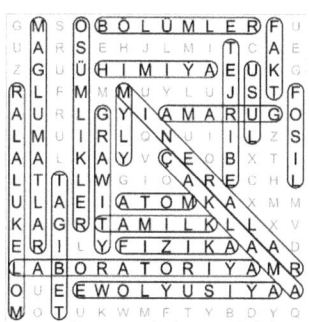

36 - Beauty

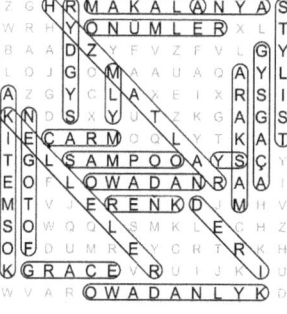

37 - Clothes

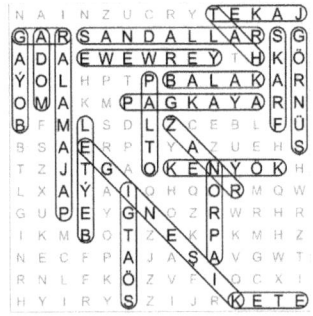

38 - Ethics

39 - Insects

40 - Astronomy

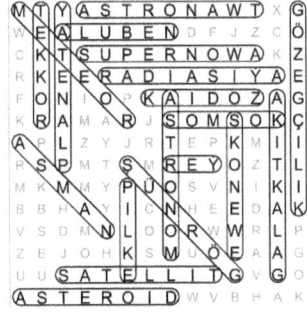

41 - Health and Wellness #2

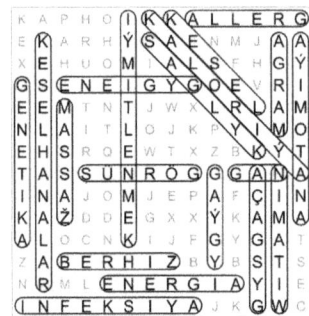

42 - Time

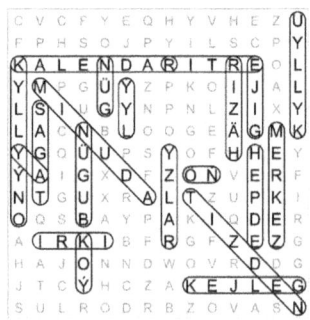

43 - Buildings

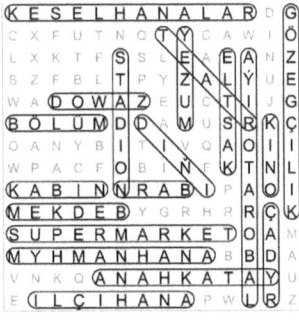

44 - Philanthropy

45 - Gardening

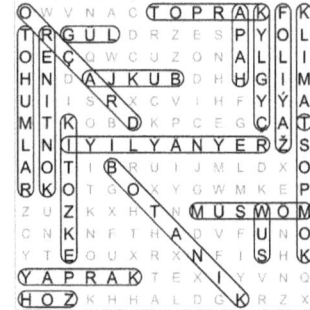

46 - Herbalism

47 - Vehicles

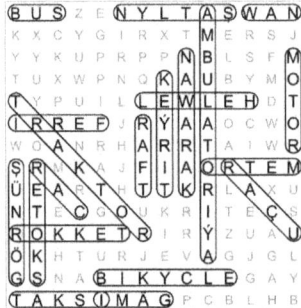

48 - Flowers

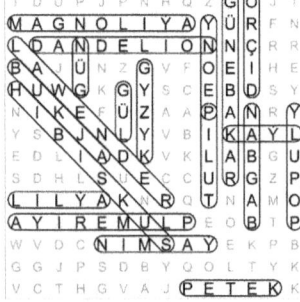

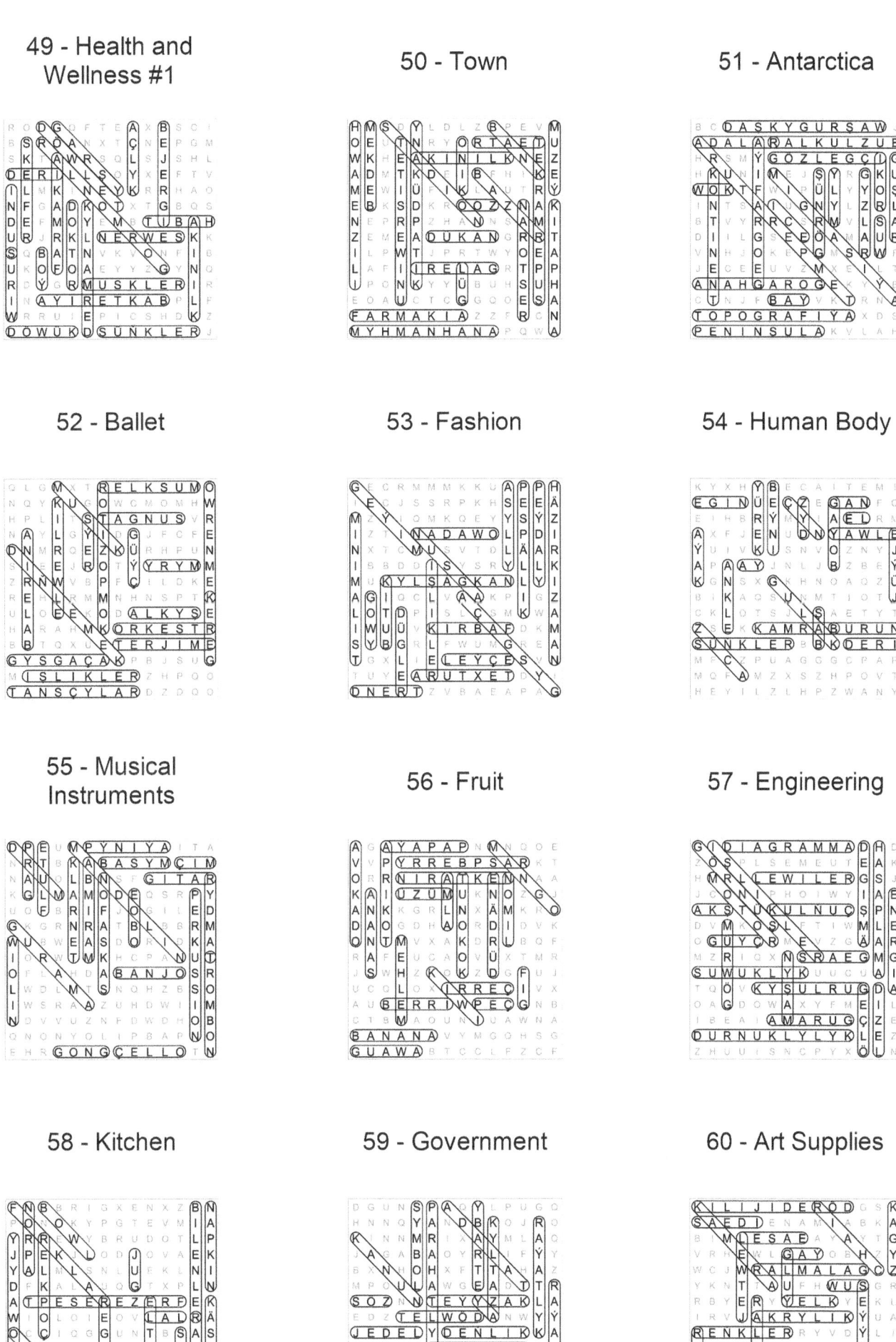

49 - Health and Wellness #1

50 - Town

51 - Antarctica

52 - Ballet

53 - Fashion

54 - Human Body

55 - Musical Instruments

56 - Fruit

57 - Engineering

58 - Kitchen

59 - Government

60 - Art Supplies

61 - Science Fiction

62 - Geometry

63 - Creativity

64 - Airplanes

65 - Ocean

66 - Force and Gravity

67 - Birds

68 - Nutrition

69 - Hiking

70 - Professions #1

71 - Barbecues

72 - Chocolate

73 - Vegetables

74 - Boats

75 - Activities and Leisure

76 - Driving

77 - Professions #2

78 - Mythology

79 - Hair Types

80 - Furniture

81 - Garden

82 - Diplomacy

83 - Countries #1

84 - Adjectives #1

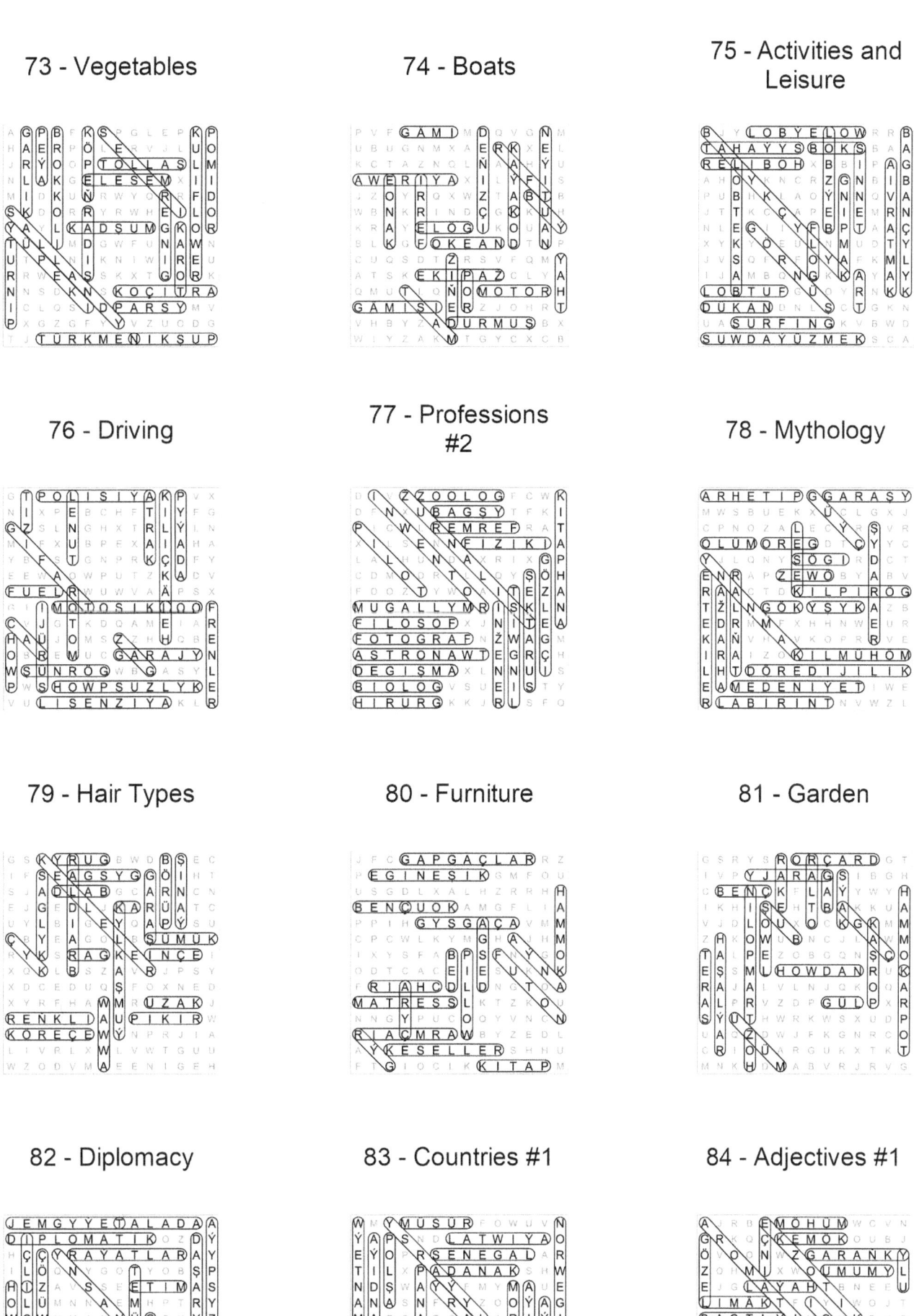

85 - Technology

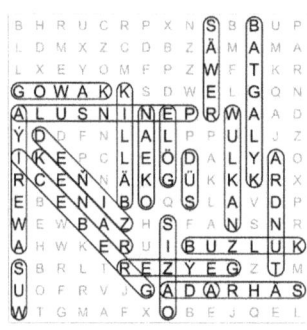

86 - Landscapes

87 - Visual Arts

88 - Plants

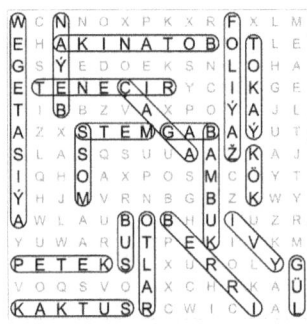

89 - Countries #2

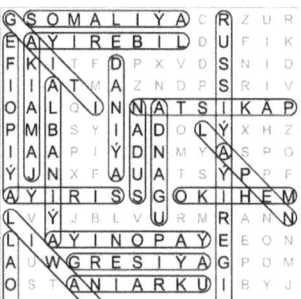

90 - Adjectives #2

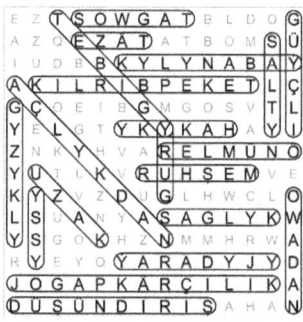

91 - Math

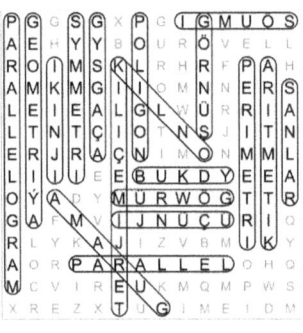

92 - Water

93 - Activities

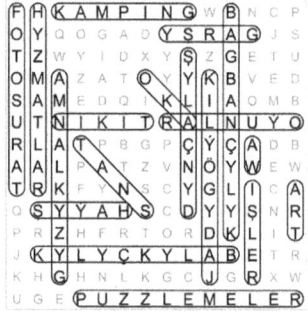

94 - Business

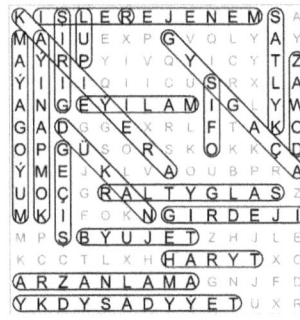

95 - Literature

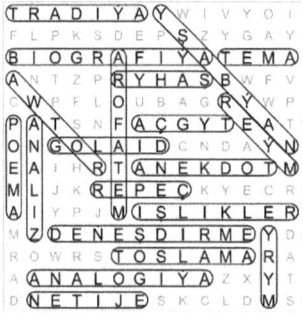

96 - Geography

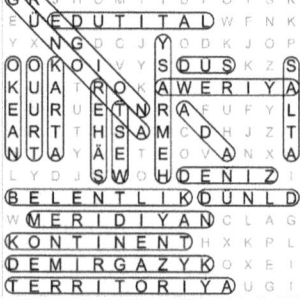

97 - Pets

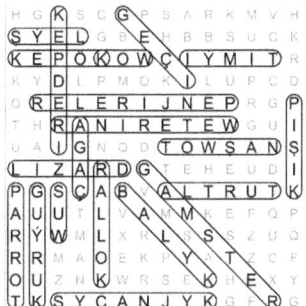

98 - Jazz

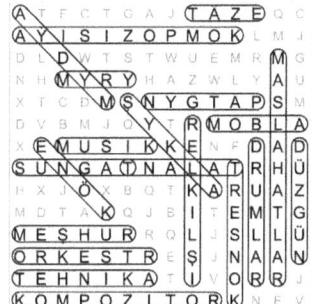

99 - Nature

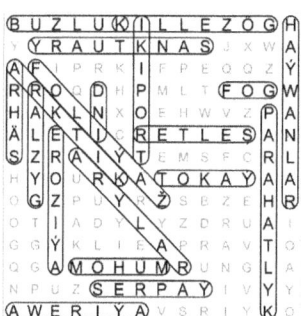

100 - Vacation #2

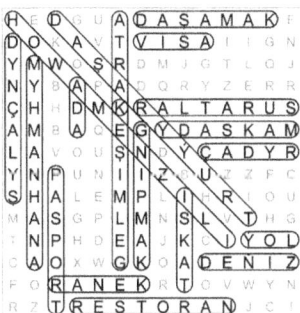

Dictionary

Activities
Çäreler

Activity	Işler
Art	Art
Camping	Kamping
Crafts	Hyzmatlar
Dancing	Tans
Fishing	Balykçylyk
Games	Oýunlar
Gardening	Bagbançylyk
Hunting	Aw
Interests	Gyzyklanma
Leisure	Dynç Alyş
Magic	Jadygöýlik
Photography	Fotosurat
Pleasure	Haýyş
Puzzles	Puzzlemeler
Reading	Oka
Relaxation	Garşy
Sewing	Tikin
Skill	Öwrenmek

Activities and Leisure
Çäreler we Dynç Alyş

Art	Art
Baseball	Beýzbol
Basketball	Basketbol
Boxing	Boks
Camping	Kamping
Diving	Aivratmak
Fishing	Balykçylyk
Gardening	Bagbançylyk
Golf	Golf
Hobbies	Hobiler
Relaxing	Görnüş
Shopping	Dükan
Soccer	Futbol
Surfing	Surfing
Swimming	Suwda Ýüzmek
Tennis	Tennis
Travel	Syýahat
Volleyball	Woleýbol

Adjectives #1
Sypatlar # 1

Absolute	Absolýut
Aromatic	Aromatik
Artistic	Sungat
Attractive	Gözel
Dark	Garaňky
Exotic	Ekzotik
Generous	Umumy
Happy	Bagtly
Heavy	Gowy
Helpful	Kömek
Honest	Ion Gowy
Huge	Uly
Identical	Birmeňzeş
Important	Möhüm
Modern	Häzirki Zaman
Perfect	Kämil
Serious	Agras
Slow	Haýal
Thin	Inçe
Valuable	Gymmat

Adjectives #2
Sypatlar # 2

Authentic	Hakyky
Creative	Ýaradyjy
Descriptive	Düşündiriş
Dry	Gury ..
Elegant	Owadan
Famous	Meşhur
Gifted	Sowgat
Healthy	Saglyk
Hot	Yssy
Hungry	Açlykdan
Interesting	Gyzykly
Natural	Tebigy
New	Täze
Productive	Önümler
Proud	Tekepbirlik
Responsible	Jogapkärçilik
Salty	Salty
Sleepy	Uzak
Strong	Güýçli
Wild	Ýabanylyk

Adventure
Başdan Geçirmeler

Activity	Işler
Beauty	Gözellik
Chance	Şans
Dangerous	Howply
Destination	Maksady
Difficulty	Kynlyk
Enthusiasm	Joşgunlylyk
Excursion	Görnüş
Friends	Dostlar
Itinerary	Syýahat
Joy	Şatlyk
Nature	Tebigat
Navigation	Nawigasiýa
New	Täze
Opportunity	Mümkinçilik
Preparation	Taýýarlyk
Safety	Howpsuzlyk
Unusual	Adaty Däl

Airplanes
Uçarlar

Adventure	Adventure
Air	Air
Altitude	Belentlik
Atmosphere	Atmosfera
Balloon	Balon
Construction	Gurluşyk
Crew	Ekipaž
Descent	Desent
Design	Dizayn
Engine	Motor
Fuel	Fuel
Height	Boý
History	Taryh
Hydrogen	Gidrogen
Landing	Ander
Passenger	Ýolagçy
Pilot	Pilot
Propellers	Propeller
Sky	Asman
Turbulence	Türşwenlik

Algebra
Algebra

Diagram	Diagramma
Equation	Gurama
Exponent	Gysgaça
Factor	Faktor
False	Ýalan
Formula	Formula
Graph	Graf
Infinite	Infinit
Linear	Linear
Matrix	Matriks
Number	Sany
Parenthesis	Ene-Ata
Problem	Mesele
Simplify	Simönekeý
Solution	Çözüw
Solve	Çöz
Subtraction	Ewiriş
Variable	Dürli
Zero	Nol

Antarctica
Antarktida

Bay	Baý
Birds	Guşlar
Clouds	Gyzlar
Conservation	Goraghana
Continent	Kontinent
Cove	Kow
Environment	Daşky Gurşaw
Expedition	Görnüş
Geography	Geografiýa
Glaciers	Buzluklar
Ice	Ice
Islands	Adalar
Migration	Migrasiýa
Peninsula	Peninsula
Researcher	Gözlegçi
Rocky	Roki
Scientific	Ylym
Temperature	Temperatura
Topography	Topografiýa
Water	Suw

Antiques
Gadymy Zatlar

Art	Art
Auction	Auksion
Authentic	Hakyky
Century	Merkez
Coins	Teňňeler
Decades	Kararlar
Decorative	Bezeg
Elegant	Owadan
Furniture	Öý Goşlary
Gallery	Galeri
Investment	Maýa Goýum
Jewelry	Ewewreý
Old	Köne
Price	Baha
Quality	Häsiýet
Restoration	Dikeldiş
Sculpture	Mekdep
Style	Işlikler
Unusual	Adaty Däl
Value	Gymmat

Archeology
Arheologiýa

Analysis	Analiz
Antiquity	Antikuity
Bones	Süňkler
Civilization	Göwrelilik
Descendant	Nesip
Era	Ermen
Evaluation	Bahalanmak
Expert	Ekspert
Fossil	Fosil
Mystery	Syr
Objects	Object
Relic	Relik
Researcher	Gözlegçi
Team	Komanda
Temple	Ybadathana
Tomb	Mazary
Unknown	Näbelli
Years	Ýyllar

Art Supplies
Sungat Enjamlary

Acrylic	Akrylik
Brushes	Bişler
Camera	Kamera
Chair	Chair
Clay	Kleý
Colors	Reňkler
Creativity	Döredijilik
Easel	Easel
Eraser	Seýýäs
Glue	Gluý
Ideas	Ideas
Ink	Ink
Oil	Ýag
Paper	Kagyz
Pencils	Galamlar
Table	Jetwel
Water	Suw
Watercolors	Suwlar

Astronomy
Astronomiýa

Asteroid	Asteroid
Astronaut	Astronawt
Astronomer	Astronom
Constellation	Görnüş
Cosmos	Kosmos
Earth	Ýer
Eclipse	Eklip
Equinox	Ewenoks
Galaxy	Galaktika
Meteor	Meteor
Moon	Ay
Nebula	Nebula
Observatory	Gözegçilik
Planet	Planeta
Radiation	Radiasiýa
Rocket	Rokket
Satellite	Satellit
Sky	Asman
Supernova	Supernowa
Zodiac	Zodiak

Ballet
Balet

Applause	Alkyş
Artistic	Sungat
Audience	Diňlemek
Ballerina	Balerina
Choreography	Horeografiýa
Composer	Kompozitor
Dancers	Tansçylar
Expressive	Gysgaça
Gesture	Elwerlik
Graceful	Gerek
Intensity	Güýç
Muscles	Muskler
Music	Musik
Orchestra	Orkestr
Practice	Terjime
Rehearsal	Reýs
Rhythm	Yrym
Skill	Öwrenmek
Style	Işlikler
Technique	Tehnika

Barbecues
Barbekues

Chicken	Çik
Children	Çagalar
Family	Maşgala
Food	Iýmit
Forks	Forklar
Friends	Dostlar
Fruit	Miwe
Games	Oýunlar
Grill	Grill
Hot	Yssy
Hunger	Açlyk
Knives	Bilenler
Music	Musik
Onions	Sogan
Salads	Saladlar
Salt	Duz
Sauce	Sçýs
Summer	Tomus
Tomatoes	Pomidorlar
Vegetables	Görnüşler

Beauty
Gözellik

Charm	Çarm
Color	Reňk
Cosmetics	Kosmetika
Curls	Kelleler
Elegance	Owadanlyk
Elegant	Owadan
Fragrance	Ys
Grace	Grace
Makeup	Makala
Mascara	Maskara
Mirror	Aýna
Photogenic	Fotogen
Products	Önümler
Scent	Ylm
Scissors	Gysgaça
Services	Hyzmatlar
Shampoo	Şampoo
Skin	Deri
Smooth	Sygdyr
Stylist	Stylist

Bees
Arylar

Beneficial	Peýdaly
Blossom	Gül
Diversity	Aivratynlyk
Ecosystem	Ekosiýon
Flowers	Güller
Food	Iýmit
Fruit	Miwe
Garden	Bag
Habitat	Habitat
Hive	Aiw
Honey	Pul
Insect	Inseksiýa
Plants	Ösümlikler
Pollen	Polen
Pollinator	Tozduryjy
Queen	Sorag
Smoke	Çilim
Sun	Gün
Swarm	Swarm
Wax	Wax

Birds
Guşlar

Canary	Kanary
Chicken	Çik
Crow	Krow
Cuckoo	Kekwoý
Dove	Dowel
Duck	Ördek
Eagle	Bürgüt
Egg	Ýumurtga
Flamingo	Flamingo
Goose	Goý
Heron	Geron
Ostrich	Ostrih
Parrot	Parrot
Peacock	Peç
Pelican	Pelikan
Penguin	Penguen
Sparrow	Serçe
Stork	Habar
Swan	Swan
Toucan	Toukan

Boats
Gämiler

Anchor	Gämi
Buoy	Buý
Canoe	Kanoe
Crew	Ekipaž
Dock	Dok
Engine	Motor
Ferry	Ferri
Kayak	Kaýak
Lake	Göle
Lifeboat	Durmuş
Mast	Mast
Nautical	Nautiýen
Ocean	Okean
Raft	Raft
River	Aweriýa
Rope	Rop
Sailboat	Gämisi
Sailor	Deňizçi
Sea	Deňiz
Yacht	Ýaht

Books
Kitaplar

Adventure	Adventure
Author	Awtor
Collection	Kolhoz
Context	Konteks
Duality	Ikilik
Epic	Epik
Historical	Taryh
Humorous	Gülki
Inventive	Terjime
Literary	Edebi
Narrator	Naýbaşy
Novel	Çeper
Page	Sahypa
Poem	Poema
Poetry	Goşgy
Reader	Okyjy
Relevant	Görnüş
Series	Series
Story	Hekaýa
Tragic	Tragik

Buildings
Jaýlar

Apartment	Bölüm
Barn	Barn
Cabin	Kabin
Castle	Kastle
Cinema	Kino
Embassy	Ilçihana
Factory	Zawod
Hospital	Keselhanalar
Hostel	Yatakhana
Hotel	Myhmanhana
Laboratory	Laboratoriýa
Museum	Muzeý
Observatory	Gözegçilik
School	Mekdeb
Stadium	Stadion
Supermarket	Supermarket
Tent	Çadyr
Theater	Teatr
Tower	Diňi
University	Uniwersitet

Business
Işewürlik

Budget	Býujet
Career	Kariýera
Company	Kompaniýa
Cost	Haryt
Currency	Gysgaça
Discount	Arzanlama
Economics	Ykdysadyýet
Employer	Işler
Factory	Zawod
Finance	Maliýe
Income	Giriş
Investment	Maýa Goýum
Manager	Menejer
Money	Pul
Office	Ofis
Profit	Girdeji
Sale	Satlyk
Shop	Dükan
Taxes	Salgytlar
Transaction	Geçiş

Camping
Kemping

Adventure	Adventure
Animals	Haýwanlar
Cabin	Kabin
Canoe	Kanoe
Compass	Kompas
Fire	Ýangyn
Forest	Tokaý
Fun	Gülki
Hammock	Hammok
Hat	Hat
Hunting	Aw
Insect	Inseksiýa
Lake	Göle
Map	Karta
Moon	Ay
Mountain	Düş
Nature	Tebigat
Rope	Rop
Tent	Çadyr
Trees	Agaçlar

Chemistry
Himiýa

Acid	Kislota
Alkaline	Alkaline
Atomic	Atom
Carbon	Karbon
Catalyst	Katalyst
Chlorine	Hlorin
Electron	Elektron
Enzyme	Enzim
Gas	Gaz
Heat	Atylylyk
Hydrogen	Gidrogen
Ion	Ion
Liquid	Suwuklyk
Molecule	Molekulýar
Nuclear	Ucadro
Organic	Organik
Oxygen	Oksigen
Salt	Duz
Temperature	Temperatura
Weight	Agram

Chocolate
Şokolad

Antioxidant	Antioksidant
Artisanal	Sungat
Bitter	Ajy
Cacao	Kakao
Calories	Kaloriýalar
Caramel	Karamel
Coconut	Kokonut
Delicious	Tagamly
Exotic	Ekzotik
Favorite	Halaýan
Ingredient	Ingredient
Peanuts	Peýdaly
Powder	Güýç
Quality	Häsiýet
Recipe	Resept
Sugar	Şeker
Sweet	Süýji
Taste	Tagam

Circus
Sirk

Acrobat	Akrobat
Animals	Haýwanlar
Balloons	Balonlar
Clown	Kloun
Costume	Kostum
Juggler	Juggler
Lion	Ýolbars
Magic	Jadygöýlik
Magician	Jadygöý
Monkey	Pul
Music	Musik
Parade	Parade
Show	Görkez
Spectator	Spektor
Tent	Çadyr
Ticket	Bilik
Tiger	Gaplaň
Trick	Hile

Clothes
Egin-Eşik

Apron	Apron
Belt	Beýtel
Blouse	Gar
Bracelet	Görnüş
Coat	Palto
Dress	Egin-Eşik
Fashion	Moda
Hat	Hat
Jacket	Jaket
Jeans	Žanr
Jewelry	Ewewreý
Necklace	Boýag
Pajamas	Pajamalar
Pants	Balak
Sandals	Sandallar
Scarf	Skarf
Shirt	Köýnek
Shoe	Aýakgap
Skirt	Etek
Sweater	Söatgi

Colors
Reňkler

Azure	Azure
Beige	Beýj
Black	Gar
Blue	Gök
Brown	Garaş
Cyan	Çýan
Fuchsia	Fuçsiya
Green	Ýaşyl
Grey	Çýk
Magenta	Magenta
Orange	Oňolga
Pink	Pembe
Purple	Püre-Pür
Red	Gyzyl
Sepia	Seýdiýa
Violet	Violet
White	Ak
Yellow	Saryk

Countries #1
1-nji Ýurt

Brazil	Braziliýa
Canada	Kanada
Egypt	Müsür
Finland	Finlandiýa
Germany	Germaniýa
Iraq	Yrak
Israel	Ysraýyl
Italy	Italýa
Latvia	Latwiýa
Libya	Libiýa
Morocco	Morokko
Nicaragua	Nikaragua
Norway	Norwegiýa
Panama	Panama
Poland	Polşa
Romania	Rumyniýa
Senegal	Senegal
Spain	Ispaniýa
Venezuela	Wenezuela
Vietnam	Wýetnam

Countries #2
2-nji Ýurt

Albania	Albaniýa
Denmark	Daniýa
Ethiopia	Efiopiýa
Greece	Gresiýa
Haiti	Gaiti
Jamaica	Jamaika
Japan	Ýaponiýa
Laos	Laos
Lebanon	Liwan
Liberia	Liberiýa
Mexico	Mehiko
Nepal	Nepal
Nigeria	Nigeriýa
Pakistan	Päkistan
Russia	Russiýa
Somalia	Somaliýa
Sudan	Sudan
Syria	Siriýa
Uganda	Uganda
Ukraine	Ukraina

Creativity
Döredijilik

Artistic	Sungat
Authenticity	Hukuk
Clarity	Garşy
Dramatic	Dramatik
Emotions	Duýgular
Fluidity	Söugi
Ideas	Ideas
Image	Surat
Imagination	Görnüş
Inspiration	Ylham
Intensity	Güýç
Intuition	Intuisiýa
Inventive	Terjime
Sensation	Sensasiýa
Skill	Öwrenmek
Spontaneous	Öz-Özünden
Visions	Görüşler
Vitality	Witaliý

Dance
Tans

Academy	Akademiýa
Art	Art
Body	Beden
Choreography	Horeografiýa
Classical	Klassyky
Culture	Medeniýet
Emotion	Duýgy
Expressive	Gysgaça
Grace	Grace
Joyful	Şatlyk
Movement	Köňli
Music	Musik
Partner	Hyzmatdaş
Posture	Surat
Rehearsal	Reýs
Rhythm	Yrym
Traditional	Söwda
Visual	Wisual

Days and Months
Günler we Aýlar

April	Aprel
August	Awgust
Calendar	Kalendar
February	Fewral
Friday	Juma Güni
January	Ýanwar
July	Iýul
March	Mart
May	Magtymguly
Monday	Duşenbe
Month	Ay
November	Noýabr
October	Oktýabr
Saturday	Şenbe
September	Ruhnam
Sunday	Ýekşenbe
Tuesday	Sişenbe
Wednesday	Çarşenbe
Week	Hepde
Year	Ýyl

Diplomacy
Diplomatiýa

Adviser	Maslahatçy
Ambassador	Ilçi
Citizens	Raýatlar
Civic	Raýat
Community	Jemgyýet
Cooperation	Hyzmatdaşlyk
Diplomatic	Diplomatik
Discussion	Jedel
Embassy	Ilçihana
Ethics	Etim
Foreign	Daşary Ýurt
Government	Hökümet
Humanitarian	Ynsan
Integrity	Aýypsyzlyk
Justice	Adalat
Politics	Politik
Resolution	Çözgüt
Security	Howpsuzlyk
Solution	Çözüw
Treaty	Terjime

Driving
Sürüji

Accident	Heläkçilik
Brakes	Frenler
Car	Car
Danger	Howp
Driver	Sürüji
Fuel	Fuel
Garage	Garajy
Gas	Gaz
License	Lisenziýa
Map	Karta
Motor	Motor
Motorcycle	Motosikl
Pedestrian	Pyýada
Police	Polisiýa
Road	Ool
Safety	Howpsuzlyk
Speed	Tiz
Traffic	Trafig
Truck	Görnüş
Tunnel	Tunel

Energy
Energetika

Battery	Batareýa
Carbon	Karbon
Diesel	Dizel
Electric	Elektrik
Electron	Elektron
Entropy	Giriş
Environment	Daşky Gurşaw
Fuel	Fuel
Gasoline	Benzin
Heat	Atylylyk
Hydrogen	Gidrogen
Industry	Sanatçylyk
Motor	Motor
Nuclear	Ucadro
Photon	Foton
Pollution	Hapalanma
Renewable	Durnuklylyk
Steam	Buhar
Turbine	Turbina
Wind	Şemal

Engineering
In Engineeringenerçilik

Angle	Işlikler
Axis	Akş
Calculation	Hasaplama
Construction	Gurluşyk
Depth	Çuňluk
Diagram	Diagramma
Diameter	Göwrüm
Diesel	Dizel
Distribution	Degişmä
Energy	Energi .a
Gears	Gears
Levers	Lewiler
Liquid	Suwuklyk
Machine	Maşyn
Measurement	Ölçeg
Motor	Motor
Propulsion	Görnüş
Stability	Durnuklylyk
Strength	Güýç
Structure	Gurama

Ethics
Etika

Altruism	Altruizm
Compassion	Garşy
Cooperation	Hyzmatdaşlyk
Dignity	Mertebe
Diplomatic	Diplomatik
Honesty	Päklik
Humanity	Adamzat
Individualism	Individualizm
Integrity	Aýypsyzlyk
Kindness	Mähirlilik
Optimism	Optimizm
Patience	Sabyrlylyk
Philosophy	Filosofiýa
Rationality	Rasallyk
Realism	Realizm
Reasonable	Maslahat
Respectful	Hormat
Tolerance	Tolgunmak
Values	Gymmatlar
Wisdom	Pähim

Family
Maşgala

Ancestor	Ata-Baba
Aunt	Daýza
Brother	Dogan
Childhood	Çaga
Children	Çagalar
Cousin	Gysgaça
Daughter	Gyzy
Father	Ata
Grandfather	Bababababa
Grandmother	Mama
Grandson	Agtygy
Husband	Är
Maternal	Enelik
Mother	Eje
Nephew	Nephew
Niece	Nieýs
Paternal	Paternal
Sister	Uýa
Uncle	Daýym
Wife	Aýal

Farm #1
1-nji Ferma

Agriculture	Ekerançylyk
Bee	Beý
Bison	Bizon
Calf	Kalf
Cat	Pişik
Chicken	Çik
Cow	Kow
Crow	Krow
Dog	Köpek
Donkey	Eşek
Fence	Kaýs
Fertilizer	Teneçir
Field	Söelgi
Goat	Geçi
Hay	Haý
Honey	Pul
Horse	At
Rice	Çigit
Seeds	Tohumlar
Water	Suw

Farm #2
2-nji Ferma

Animals	Haýwanlar
Barley	Arpa
Barn	Barn
Beehive	Beýiw
Corn	Korn
Duck	Ördek
Farmer	Fermer
Food	Iýmit
Fruit	Miwe
Irrigation	Suwaryş
Lamb	Guzy
Llama	Llama
Meadow	Meýadow
Milk	Süýt
Orchard	Orçard
Sheep	Goýun
Tractor	Traktor
Vegetable	Bäşgä
Wheat	Bugdaý
Windmill	Windmill

Fashion
Moda

Affordable	Gowy
Boutique	Butik
Buttons	Dügler
Clothing	Geýim
Elegant	Owadan
Embroidery	Nakgaşlyk
Expensive	Gysgaça
Fabric	Fabrik
Lace	Leýçe
Minimalist	Minimalist
Modern	Häzirki Zaman
Modest	Pespällik
Original	Asylly
Pattern	Nusga
Practical	Peýdaly
Style	Işlikler
Texture	Textura
Trend	Trend

Fishing
Balyk Tutmak

Bait	Baýt
Basket	Basym
Beach	Kenar
Boat	Gämi
Cook	Kok
Equipment	Gurnama
Exaggeration	Gysgaçaçlyk
Fins	Fins
Gills	Gill
Hook	Huk
Jaw	Jüýje
Lake	Göle
Ocean	Okean
Patience	Sabyrlylyk
River	Aweriýa
Season	Möwsüm
Water	Suw
Weight	Agram
Wire	Wir

Flowers
Güller

Bouquet	Bukja
Clover	Gyzyk
Daisy	Gün
Dandelion	Dandelion
Gardenia	Bagban
Hibiscus	Hibiskus
Jasmine	Ýasmin
Lavender	Lawender
Lilac	Lýak
Lily	Lilýa
Magnolia	Magnoliýa
Orchid	Orçid
Peony	Peony
Petal	Petek
Plumeria	Plumeriya
Poppy	Populy
Rose	Gül
Sunflower	Günebakar
Tulip	Tulip

Food #1
Iýmit # 1

Apricot	Aprikot
Barley	Arpa
Basil	Basil
Carrot	Karot
Cinnamon	Sinnamon
Garlic	Garlik
Juice	Şire
Lemon	Limon
Milk	Süýt
Onion	Köpeň
Peanut	Arahis
Pear	Dürdäne
Salad	Sallandy
Salt	Duz
Soup	Çorbasy
Spinach	Ýüpeki
Strawberry	Samançy
Sugar	Şeker
Tuna	Tuna
Turnip	Turnip

Food #2
Iýmit # 2

Apple	Alma
Artichoke	Artiçok
Banana	Banana
Broccoli	Brokkoli
Celery	Seleri
Cheese	Çeýe
Cherry	Çerri
Chicken	Çik
Chocolate	Şokolat
Egg	Ýumurtga
Eggplant	Mesele
Fish	Balyk
Grape	Üzüm
Ham	Ham
Kiwi	Kiwi
Mushroom	Muşdak
Rice	Çigit
Tomato	Pomidor
Wheat	Bugdaý
Yogurt	Ýogurt

Force and Gravity
Güýç we Agyrlyk Güýji

Axis	Akş
Center	Merkez
Discovery	Açyş
Distance	Aralyk
Dynamic	Ind
Expansion	Giňeldiş
Friction	Çekişme
Impact	Täsirlilik
Magnetism	Magnetizm
Mechanics	Mexanika
Orbit	Orbit
Physics	Fizika
Pressure	Basyş
Properties	Häsiýetler
Speed	Tiz
Time	Wagt
Universal	Universal
Weight	Agram

Fruit
Miwe

Apple	Alma
Apricot	Aprikot
Avocado	Avokado
Banana	Banana
Berry	Berri
Cherry	Çerri
Coconut	Kokonut
Fig	Fig
Grape	Üzüm
Guava	Guawa
Kiwi	Kiwi
Lemon	Limon
Mango	Mango
Melon	Melhem
Nectarine	Nektarin
Papaya	Papaýa
Peach	Peç
Pear	Dürdäne
Pineapple	Ananas
Raspberry	Raspberry

Furniture
Mebel

Armchair	Armçair
Bed	Bed
Bench	Benç
Bookcase	Kitap
Chair	Chair
Couch	Kouç
Curtains	Gysgaça
Cushions	Keseller
Desk	Desga
Dresser	Egin-Eşik
Futon	Futon
Hammock	Hammok
Lamp	Çyra
Mattress	Matress
Mirror	Aýna
Pillow	Pillow
Rug	Rýg
Shelves	Gap-Gaçlar

Garden
Bag

Bench	Benç
Bush	Buş
Fence	Kaýs
Flower	Gül
Garage	Garajy
Garden	Bag
Grass	Otlar
Hammock	Hammok
Hose	Hoz
Orchard	Orçard
Pond	Howdan
Porch	Porşak
Rake	Rake
Shovel	Şowel
Soil	Toprak
Terrace	Teras
Trampoline	Trampolin
Tree	Agaç
Vine	Üzüm
Weeds	Haşalýar

Gardening
Bagçylyk

Blossom	Gül
Botanical	Botanik
Bouquet	Bukja
Climate	Klimat
Compost	Kompost
Container	Kontiner
Dirt	Hapa
Edible	Iýilýän Ýer
Exotic	Ekzotik
Foliage	Foliýaž
Hose	Hoz
Leaf	Ýaprak
Moisture	Çyglyk
Orchard	Orçard
Seasonal	Möwsüm
Seeds	Tohumlar
Soil	Toprak
Water	Suw

Geography
Geografiýa

Altitude	Belentlik
Atlas	Atlas
City	Şäher
Continent	Kontinent
Country	Ouurt
Hemisphere	Hemrasy
Island	Ada
Latitude	Latitude
Map	Karta
Meridian	Meridiýan
Mountain	Düş
North	Demirgazyk
Ocean	Okean
Region	Region
River	Aweriýa
Sea	Deňiz
South	Günorta
Territory	Territoriýa
West	West
World	Dünld

Geology
Geologiýa

Acid	Kislota
Calcium	Kalsiý
Cavern	Kawern
Continent	Kontinent
Coral	Koral
Crystals	Gyzyklar
Cycles	Syklar
Earthquake	Arter
Erosion	Eroziýa
Fossil	Fosil
Geyser	Geýzer
Lava	Lava
Layer	Gatlak
Minerals	Mineralar
Plateau	Plateo
Quartz	Kwars
Salt	Duz
Stalactite	Stalaktit
Stone	Daş
Volcano	Wulkan

Geometry
Geometriýa

Angle	Işlikler
Calculation	Hasaplama
Circle	Däbiň
Curve	Egri
Diameter	Göwrüm
Dimension	Ölçeg
Equation	Gurama
Height	Boý
Horizontal	Gorizontal
Logic	Logik
Mass	Massaly
Median	Median
Number	Sany
Parallel	Parallel
Proportion	Ösüş
Segment	Bölüm
Surface	Daşky
Symmetry	Symmetri
Theory	Teoriýa
Triangle	Üçünji

Government
Hökümet

Citizenship	Raýatlyk
Civil	Raýat
Constitution	Konstitusiýa
Democracy	Demokratiýa
Discussion	Jedel
District	Etraby
Equality	Deňlik
Independence	Garaşsyzlyk
Judicial	Kazyýet
Justice	Adalat
Law	Kanun
Leader	Ýolbaşçy
Liberty	Azatlyk
Monument	Ay
Nation	Milli
Peaceful	Parahatlyk
Politics	Politik
Speech	Söz
State	Döwlet
Symbol	Symbol

Hair Types
Saç Görnüşleri

Bald	Bald
Black	Gar
Braided	Börüp
Braids	Braidlar
Brown	Garaş
Colored	Reňkli
Curls	Kelleler
Curly	Köreçe
Dry	Gury ..
Gray	Çyk
Healthy	Saglyk
Long	Uzak
Shiny	Şinaý
Short	Gysga
Silver	Kümüş
Soft	Ýumşaklyk
Thick	Pikir
Thin	Inçe
Wavy	Wawwa
White	Ak

Health and Wellness #1
Saglyk we Saglyk # 1

Active	Indus
Bacteria	Bakteriýa
Bones	Süňkler
Clinic	Klinika
Doctor	Doktor
Fracture	Döwük
Habit	Habit
Height	Boý
Hormones	Gormonlar
Hunger	Açlyk
Medicine	Dermanlyk
Muscles	Muskler
Nerves	Nerwes
Pharmacy	Farmaki .a
Reflex	Refleks
Relaxation	Garşy
Skin	Deri
Therapy	Bejergi
Treatment	Döwlet
Virus	Wirus

Health and Wellness #2
Saglyk we Saglyk # 2

Allergy	Allerg
Anatomy	Anatomiýa
Appetite	Görnüş
Blood	Gan
Calorie	Kaloriýa
Dehydration	Gysgaça
Diet	Berhiz
Disease	Kesel
Energy	Energi .a
Genetics	Genetika
Healthy	Saglyk
Hospital	Keselhanalar
Hygiene	Gygiene
Infection	Infeksiya
Massage	Massaž
Nutrition	Iýmitlenmek
Recovery	Terjime
Stress	Gaýgy
Vitamin	Witamin
Weight	Agram

Herbalism
Gerbalizm

Aromatic	Aromatik
Basil	Basil
Beneficial	Peýdaly
Culinary	Kulinary
Fennel	Fennel
Flavor	Tagam
Flower	Gül
Garden	Bag
Garlic	Garlik
Green	Ýaşyl
Ingredient	Ingredient
Lavender	Lawender
Marjoram	Marjoram
Mint	Mont
Oregano	Oregano
Parsley	Parsy
Plant	Zawod
Rosemary	Rozymary
Saffron	Şafron
Tarragon	Tarragon

Hiking
Gezelenç

Animals	Haýwanlar
Boots	Aýakgap
Camping	Kamping
Cliff	Kliff
Climate	Klimat
Guides	Gollanmalar
Heavy	Gowy
Map	Karta
Mountain	Düş
Nature	Tebigat
Orientation	Gaýşat
Parks	Parklar
Preparation	Taýýarlyk
Stones	Daşlar
Summit	Sammit
Sun	Gün
Tired	Ýadaw
Water	Suw
Weather	Howa
Wild	Ýabanylyk

House
Jaý

Attic	Attik
Broom	Garaş
Curtains	Gysgaça
Door	Gapy
Fence	Kaýs
Fireplace	Ojak
Floor	Gül
Furniture	Öý Goşlary
Garage	Garajy
Garden	Bag
Keys	Açarylar
Kitchen	Kitçen
Lamp	Çyra
Library	Kitaphana
Mirror	Aýna
Roof	Roof
Room	Otag
Shower	Duş
Wall	Wall
Window	Ewez

Human Body
Adam Bedeni

Ankle	Ankle
Blood	Gan
Bones	Süñkler
Brain	Beýni
Chin	Çyn
Ear	Gulak
Elbow	Elwaý
Face	Acüz
Finger	Barmak
Hand	El
Head	Baş
Heart	Ýürek
Jaw	Jüýje
Knee	Dyz
Leg	Aýak
Mouth	Ay
Neck	Boýag
Nose	Burun
Shoulder	Egin
Skin	Deri

Insects
Mör-Möjekler

Ant	Ant
Aphid	Aphid
Bee	Beý
Beetle	Beýtla
Butterfly	Sötergi
Cicada	Sikada
Cockroach	Horaz
Dragonfly	Garaşy
Flea	Fleýa
Grasshopper	Grasshopper
Hornet	Hornet
Ladybug	Zenanbug
Larva	Larwa
Locust	Lokust
Mantis	Antis
Mosquito	Bogunlar
Moth	Eje
Termite	Termit
Wasp	Wasp
Worm	Iş

Jazz
Jaz

Album	Albom
Applause	Alkyş
Artist	Sungat
Composer	Kompozitor
Composition	Kompozisiýa
Concert	Konsert
Drums	Drumlar
Emphasis	Nygtap
Famous	Meşhur
Favorites	Maslahatlar
Improvisation	Düzgün
Music	Musik
New	Täze
Old	Köne
Orchestra	Orkestr
Rhythm	Yrym
Song	Aýdym
Style	Işlikler
Talent	Talant
Technique	Tehnika

Kitchen
Aşhana

Apron	Apron
Bowl	Bowl
Chopsticks	Çopkler
Cups	Käseler
Food	Iýmit
Forks	Forklar
Freezer	Frezer
Grill	Grill
Jar	Jar
Jug	Jug
Kettle	Kettle
Knives	Bilenler
Ladle	Lal
Napkin	Napkin
Oven	Oven
Recipe	Resept
Refrigerator	Sowadyjy
Spices	Spices
Sponge	Sünger
Spoons	Gyzlar

Landscapes
Peýza

Beach	Kenar
Cave	Gowak
Desert	Sähra
Geyser	Geýzer
Glacier	Buzluk
Hill	Bällik
Iceberg	Iceberg
Island	Ada
Lake	Göle
Mountain	Düş
Oasis	Oazis
Ocean	Okean
Peninsula	Peninsula
River	Aweriýa
Sea	Deňiz
Swamp	Batgalyk
Tundra	Tundra
Valley	Säwer
Volcano	Wulkan
Waterfall	Suw

Literature
Edebiýat

Analogy	Analogiýa
Analysis	Analiz
Anecdote	Anekdot
Author	Awtor
Biography	Biografiýa
Comparison	Deňeşdirme
Conclusion	Netije
Description	Açgyt
Dialogue	Dialog
Fiction	Toslama
Metaphor	Metafora
Narrator	Naýbaşy
Novel	Çeper
Poem	Poema
Poetic	Şahyr
Rhyme	Reým
Rhythm	Yrym
Style	Işlikler
Theme	Tema
Tragedy	Tradiýa

Mammals
Süýdemdirijiler

Bear	Aýy
Beaver	Beawer
Bull	Öküz
Camel	Düýe
Cat	Pişik
Coyote	Koyot
Dog	Köpek
Dolphin	Delfin
Fox	Tilki
Giraffe	Girew
Gorilla	Gorilla
Horse	At
Kangaroo	Kangýuý
Lion	Ýolbars
Monkey	Pul
Rabbit	Towşan
Sheep	Goýun
Whale	Balina
Wolf	Möjek
Zebra	Zebra

Math
Matematika

Angles	Bukdy
Arithmetic	Aritmetik
Circumference	Terjimeçilik
Decimal	Onlik
Diameter	Göwrüm
Equation	Gurama
Exponent	Gysgaça
Geometry	Geometriýa
Numbers	Sanlar
Parallel	Parallel
Parallelogram	Parallelogram
Perimeter	Perimetri
Polygon	Poligon
Rectangle	Görnüş
Square	Ikinji
Symmetry	Symmetri
Triangle	Üçünji
Volume	Söumgi

Measurements
Ölçegler

Byte	Baýt
Centimeter	Merkez
Decimal	Onlik
Degree	Gerek
Depth	Çuňluk
Gram	Gram
Height	Boý
Inch	Inç
Kilogram	Kilogram
Kilometer	Unit-Format
Length	Uzynlyk
Liter	Litr
Mass	Massaly
Minute	Minuda
Ounce	Onadamlyk
Ton	Ton
Volume	Söumgi
Weight	Agram
Width	Giňlik

Meditation
Meditasiýa

Acceptance	Kabul Etmek
Awake	Oýan
Calm	Çalyş
Clarity	Garşy
Emotions	Duýgular
Gratitude	Minnetdarlygy
Habits	Habitler
Happiness	Bagt
Kindness	Mähirlilik
Mental	Akyl
Mind	Pikir
Movement	Köňli
Music	Musik
Nature	Tebigat
Observation	Görnüş
Peace	Parahatlyk
Perspective	Şahsy .et
Posture	Surat
Silence	Dymmak
Thoughts	Pikirler

Music
Saz

Album	Albom
Ballad	Baldak
Chorus	Hor
Classical	Klassyky
Eclectic	Eklektik
Harmonic	Garmonik
Harmony	Sazlaşyk
Lyrical	Liriki
Melody	Melodiýa
Microphone	Mikropon
Musical	Saz
Musician	Mugt
Opera	Opera
Poetic	Şahyr
Recording	Ecazgy
Rhythm	Yrym
Rhythmic	Ritm
Sing	Aýdym
Singer	Bagşy
Vocal	Vokal

Musical Instruments
Saz Gurallary

Banjo	Banjo
Bassoon	Basym
Cello	Çello
Chimes	Çim
Clarinet	Klarnet
Drum	Drum
Flute	Flute
Gong	Gong
Guitar	Gitar
Harp	Garp
Mandolin	Mandolin
Marimba	Marimba
Oboe	Oboe
Percussion	Perkussion
Piano	Pýniýa
Saxophone	Saksafon
Tambourine	Tamdyr
Trombone	Trombon
Trumpet	Gurama
Violin	Wiolin

Mythology
Mifologiýa

Archetype	Arhetip
Behavior	Sö .gi
Beliefs	Ynanmak
Creation	Rearadyş
Creature	Döredijilik
Culture	Medeniýet
Deities	Taňrlar
Disaster	Kesel
Heaven	Gök
Hero	Gero
Immortality	Möhümlik
Jealousy	Göriplik
Labyrinth	Labirint
Legend	Ertekiler
Lightning	Yşyk
Monster	Aždarha
Mortal	Ölüm
Revenge	Öwez
Strength	Güýç
Warrior	Garaşy

Nature
Tebigat

Animals	Haýwanlar
Arctic	Arktik
Beauty	Gözellik
Bees	Arylar
Clouds	Gyzlar
Desert	Sähra
Dynamic	Ind
Erosion	Eroziýa
Fog	Fog
Foliage	Foliýaž
Forest	Tokaý
Glacier	Buzluk
Peaceful	Parahatlyk
River	Aweriýa
Sanctuary	Sanktuary
Serene	Serpaý
Shelter	Şelter
Tropical	Tropiki
Vital	Möhüm
Wild	Ýabanylyk

Numbers
Sanlar

Decimal	Onlik
Eight	Sekiz
Eighteen	On Sekiz
Fifteen	Bäş
Fourteen	Dört
Math	Mat
Nine	Dokuz
Nineteen	Dokuzynjy
One	Bir
Seven	Ýedi
Seventeen	Vedinji
Six	Alty
Sixteen	Altynjy
Ten	On
Thirteen	Üçünji
Three	Üç
Twelve	Iki
Twenty	Wigrimi
Zero	Nol

Nutrition
Iýmitlenme

Appetite	Görnüş
Balanced	Balan
Bitter	Ajy
Calories	Kaloriýalar
Carbohydrates	Karbamid
Diet	Berhiz
Digestion	Siňdiriş
Edible	Iýilýän Ýer
Fermentation	Fermentasiýa
Flavor	Tagam
Habits	Habitler
Health	Saglyk
Liquids	Suwuklyklar
Nutrient	Iýmit
Proteins	Gorag
Quality	Häsiýet
Sauce	Sçýs
Toxin	Toksin
Vitamin	Witamin
Weight	Agram

Ocean
Okean

Algae	Alga
Coral	Koral
Crab	Krab
Dolphin	Delfin
Eel	Eel
Fish	Balyk
Octopus	Otrýad
Oyster	Oyster
Reef	Reýf
Salt	Duz
Seaweed	Deňiz
Shark	Şark
Shrimp	Balykemp
Sponge	Sünger
Storm	Tupan
Tides	Tides
Tuna	Tuna
Turtle	Turtla
Waves	Waves
Whale	Balina

Pets
Öý Haýwanlary

Cat	Pişik
Claws	Penjireler
Collar	Kollar
Cow	Kow
Dog	Köpek
Fish	Balyk
Food	Iýmit
Goat	Geçi
Hamster	Gamster
Kitten	Kepderi
Leash	Leýş
Lizard	Lizard
Mouse	Syçanjyk
Parrot	Parrot
Puppy	Çaga
Rabbit	Towşan
Tail	Guýruk
Turtle	Turtla
Veterinarian	Weterinar
Water	Suw

Philanthropy
Haýyr-Sahawat

Charity	Sadakalar
Children	Çagalar
Community	Jemgyýet
Contacts	Kontaktlar
Donate	Bermek
Finance	Maliýe
Funds	Fondlar
Generosity	Umumy
Goals	Maksatlar
Groups	Toparlar
History	Taryh
Honesty	Päklik
Humanity	Adamzat
Mission	Mission
Need	Gerek
People	Halk
Programs	Programmalar
Public	Senagat
Youth	Youaş

Photography
Fotosurat

Black	Gar
Camera	Kamera
Color	Reňk
Composition	Kompozisiýa
Contrast	Şertler
Darkness	Garaňkylyk
Definition	Aňlatma
Exhibition	Sergi
Format	Format
Frame	Çarçuwa
Lighting	Yşyk
Object	Maksat
Perspective	Şahsy .et
Portrait	Portret
Shadows	Kölege
Subject	Mowzuk
Texture	Textura
Visual	Wisual

Physics
Fizika

Acceleration	Tizlenme
Atom	Atom
Chaos	Kaoslyk
Chemical	Himiýa
Density	Dykyzlyk
Electron	Elektron
Engine	Motor
Formula	Formula
Frequency	Ýygym
Gas	Gaz
Magnetism	Magnetizm
Mass	Massaly
Mechanics	Mexanika
Molecule	Molekulýar
Nuclear	Ucadro
Particle	Bölüm
Relativity	Gatnaşyk
Speed	Tiz
Universal	Universal
Velocity	Terjime

Plants
Ösümlikler

Bamboo	Bambuk
Bean	Beýan
Berry	Berri
Botany	Botanika
Bush	Buş
Cactus	Kaktus
Fertilizer	Teneçir
Flora	Gül
Flower	Gül
Foliage	Foliýaž
Forest	Tokaý
Garden	Bag
Grass	Otlar
Ivy	Ivy
Moss	Moss
Petal	Petek
Root	Kök
Stem	Stem
Tree	Agaç
Vegetation	Wegetasiýa

Professions #1
Hünärler # 1

Ambassador	Ilçi
Astronomer	Astronom
Attorney	Prokuror
Banker	Bank
Cartographer	Kartograf
Coach	Komendiýa
Dancer	Tansçy
Doctor	Doktor
Editor	Editçi
Geologist	Geolog
Hunter	Awçy
Jeweler	Şaý-Sepler
Musician	Mugt
Nurse	Şepagat Uýasy
Pianist	Pýanisti
Plumber	Plumber
Psychologist	Psiholog
Sailor	Deňizçi
Tailor	Taňk
Veterinarian	Weterinar

Professions #2
Hünärler # 2

Astronaut	Astronawt
Biologist	Biolog
Dentist	Diş Lukmany
Detective	Dcgişmä
Engineer	Inžener
Farmer	Fermer
Gardener	Bagşy
Inventor	Inwentor
Journalist	Žurnalist
Librarian	Kitaphana
Linguist	Lingwist
Painter	Suratkeş
Philosopher	Filosof
Photographer	Fotograf
Physician	Fiziki
Pilot	Pilot
Researcher	Gözlegçi
Surgeon	Hirurg
Teacher	Mugallym
Zoologist	Zoolog

Science
Ylym

Atom	Atom
Chemical	Himiýa
Climate	Klimat
Data	Maglumatlar
Evolution	Ewolýusiýa
Experiment	Tejribe
Fact	Fakt
Fossil	Fosil
Gravity	Grawity
Hypothesis	Çaklama
Laboratory	Laboratoriýa
Method	Usul
Minerals	Mineralar
Molecules	Molekulalar
Nature	Tebigat
Organism	Gurama
Particles	Bölümler
Physics	Fizika
Plants	Ösümlikler
Scientist	Ylym

Science Fiction
Ylmy Fantastika

Atomic	Atom
Books	Kitaplar
Chemicals	Himikalar
Cinema	Kino
Clones	Klonlar
Dystopia	Dystopi .a
Extreme	Ewg
Fantastic	Fantastik
Fire	Ýangyn
Futuristic	Geljek
Galaxy	Galaktika
Illusion	Ilýustrasiýa
Imaginary	Görnüş
Mysterious	Syrly
Oracle	Oracle
Planet	Planeta
Robots	Robotlar
Technology	Tehnologiýa
Utopia	Utopiýa
World	Dünld

Scientific Disciplines
Ylmy Düzgünler

Anatomy	Anatomiýa
Archaeology	Arheologiýa
Astronomy	Astronomiýa
Biochemistry	Biohimiýa
Biology	Biologiýa
Botany	Botanika
Chemistry	Himiýa
Ecology	Ekologiýa
Geology	Geologiýa
Immunology	Immunologiýa
Kinesiology	Kinesiologiýa
Linguistics	Diller
Mechanics	Mexanika
Mineralogy	Mineralogý
Neurology	Newrologiýa
Physiology	Fiziologiýa
Psychology	Psihologiýa
Sociology	Jemgy .et
Thermodynamics	Termodinamika
Zoology	Zologi .a

Shapes
Şekiller

Arc	Arç
Circle	Däbiň
Cone	Kon
Corner	Burç
Cube	Kub
Curve	Egri
Cylinder	Kelle
Edges	Gaýdlar
Ellipse	Elipse
Hyperbola	Giperbola
Line	Hat
Oval	Oval
Polygon	Poligon
Prism	Prizma
Pyramid	Pýhamidi
Rectangle	Görnüş
Side	Tarap
Square	Ikinji
Triangle	Üçünji

Spices
Icesakymly Yslar

Anise	Anise
Bitter	Ajy
Cardamom	Kardamom
Cinnamon	Sinnamon
Clove	Söovgi
Coriander	Koriandr
Cumin	Jumin
Curry	Küri
Fennel	Fennel
Fenugreek	Fenugrek
Flavor	Tagam
Garlic	Garlik
Ginger	Ginger
Nutmeg	Nutmeg
Onion	Köpeň
Paprika	Paprika
Saffron	Şafron
Salt	Duz
Sweet	Süýji
Vanilla	Wanilla

Sport
Sport

Ability	Başarnyk
Athlete	Türgen
Body	Beden
Bones	Süňkler
Cardiovascular	Ýürek-Damar
Coach	Komendiýa
Cycling	Gysgaça
Dancing	Tans
Diet	Berhiz
Endurance	Çydamlylyk
Goal	Maksat
Health	Saglyk
Jogging	Jogäp
Maximize	Iň köp Adam
Metabolic	Metabolik
Muscles	Muskler
Nutrition	Iýmitlenmek
Program	Program
Sports	Sporalar
Strength	Güýç

Technology
Tehnologiýa

Blog	Blog
Browser	Görnüş
Bytes	Baýt
Camera	Kamera
Computer	Kompýuter
Cursor	Kursor
Data	Maglumatlar
Digital	Digital
File	Faýl
Font	Kalam
Internet	Internet
Message	Habar
Research	Gözleg
Screen	Ekran
Security	Howpsuzlyk
Software	Programma
Statistics	Statistika
Virtual	Wirtual
Virus	Wirus

Time
Wagt

After	Yzlar
Annual	Uyllyk
Before	Öň
Calendar	Kalendar
Century	Merkez
Day	Gün
Decade	Onýyllyk
Early	Irki
Future	Geljek
Hour	Sagat
Minute	Minuda
Month	Ay
Morning	Ertir
Night	Gije
Noon	Ýok
Now	Häzir
Soon	Tizden
Today	Bu Gün
Week	Hepde
Year	Ýyl

Town
Şäher

Airport	Howa Menzili
Bank	Bank
Bookstore	Kitap Dükany
Cinema	Kino
Clinic	Klinika
Florist	Gül
Gallery	Galeri
Hotel	Myhmanhana
Library	Kitaphana
Market	Bazar
Museum	Muzeý
Pharmacy	Farmaki .a
Restaurant	Restoran
School	Mekdeb
Stadium	Stadion
Store	Dükan
Supermarket	Supermarket
Theater	Teatr
University	Uniwersitet
Zoo	Zoo

Universe
Unilem

Asteroid	Asteroid
Astronomer	Astronom
Astronomy	Astronomiýa
Atmosphere	Atmosfera
Celestial	Kelesi
Cosmic	Kosmik
Darkness	Garaňkylyk
Eon	Eon
Galaxy	Galaktika
Hemisphere	Hemrasy
Horizon	Gonşy
Latitude	Latitude
Moon	Ay
Orbit	Orbit
Sky	Asman
Solar	Gün
Solstice	Çözgün
Telescope	Teleskop
Visible	Görniş
Zodiac	Zodiak

Vacation #2
2-nji Dynç Alyş

Airport	Howa Menzili
Beach	Kenar
Camping	Kamping
Destination	Maksady
Foreign	Daşary Ýurt
Foreigner	Gelmişek
Holiday	Baýramçylyk
Hotel	Myhmanhana
Island	Ada
Journey	Ýol
Leisure	Dynç Alyş
Map	Karta
Passport	Pasport
Photos	Suratlar
Restaurant	Restoran
Sea	Deňiz
Taxi	Taksi
Tent	Çadyr
Transportation	Daşamak
Visa	Visa

Vegetables
Gök Önümler

Artichoke	Artiçok
Broccoli	Brokkoli
Carrot	Karot
Cauliflower	Kuliflower
Celery	Seleri
Cucumber	Türkmen
Eggplant	Mesele
Garlic	Garlik
Ginger	Ginger
Mushroom	Muşdak
Onion	Köpeň
Parsley	Parsy
Pea	Peýa
Pumpkin	Puşkin
Radish	Radiş
Salad	Sallandy
Shallot	Şallot
Spinach	Ýüpeki
Tomato	Pomidor
Turnip	Turnip

Vehicles
Ulaglar

Airplane	Uçar
Ambulance	Ambulatoriýa
Bicycle	Bikycle
Boat	Gämi
Bus	Bus
Car	Car
Caravan	Karawan
Ferry	Ferri
Helicopter	Helwel
Motor	Motor
Raft	Raft
Rocket	Rokket
Scooter	Skoter
Shuttle	Şatlyn
Subway	Metro
Taxi	Taksi
Tires	Tirýek
Tractor	Traktor
Truck	Görnüş
Van	Wan

Visual Arts
Wizual Sungat

Architecture	Arhitektura
Artist	Sungatçy
Ceramics	Keramika
Chalk	Çaly ..
Charcoal	Çarkoal
Clay	Palçyk
Composition	Kompozisiýa
Creativity	Döredijilik
Easel	Easel
Film	Film
Masterpiece	Masterpiece
Painting	Görnüş
Pencil	Galam
Perspective	Şahsy .et
Photograph	Fotograf
Portrait	Portrait
Pottery	Küýzegär
Sculpture	Mekdep
Stencil	Stencil
Wax	Wax

Water
Suw

Canal	Kanal
Drinkable	Içmek
Evaporation	Buglamak
Flood	Söodgi
Frost	Aýaz
Geyser	Geyser
Humidity	Ynsanlyk
Hurricane	Gurrikan
Ice	Ice
Irrigation	Suwaryş
Lake	Lake
Moisture	Moisture
Monsoon	Monsoon
Ocean	Okean
Rain	Rain
River	River
Shower	Shower
Snow	Snow
Steam	Steam
Waves	Tolkunlar

Weather
Howa

Atmosphere	Atmosphere
Breeze	Breeze
Climate	Klimat
Cloud	Gyzyk
Drought	Görnüş
Dry	Gury ..
Fog	Duman
Hurricane	Gurrikan
Ice	Ice
Lightning	Yşyk
Monsoon	Monsoon
Polar	Polar
Rainbow	Rainbow
Sky	Sky
Storm	Hekaýa
Temperature	Temperatura
Thunder	Thunder
Tornado	Tornado
Tropical	Tropikal
Wind	Wind

Congratulations

You made it!

We hope you enjoyed this book as much as we enjoyed making it. We do our best to make high quality games.
These puzzles are designed in a clever way for you to learn actively while having fun!

Did you love them?

A Simple Request

Our books exist thanks your reviews. Could you help us by leaving one now?

Here is a short link which will take you to your order review page:

BestBooksActivity.com/Review50

MONSTER CHALLENGE!

Challenge #1

Ready for Your Bonus Game? We use them all the time but they are not so easy to find. Here are **Synonyms**!

Note 5 words you discovered in each of the Puzzles noted below (#21, #36, #76) and try to find 2 synonyms for each word.

Note 5 Words from *Puzzle 21*

Words	Synonym 1	Synonym 2

Note 5 Words from *Puzzle 36*

Words	Synonym 1	Synonym 2

Note 5 Words from *Puzzle 76*

Words	Synonym 1	Synonym 2

Challenge #2

Now that you are warmed-up, note 5 words you discovered in each Puzzle noted below (#9, #17, #25) and try to find 2 antonyms for each word.
How many lines can you do in 20 minutes?

Note 5 Words from **Puzzle 9**

Words	Antonym 1	Antonym 2

Note 5 Words from **Puzzle 17**

Words	Antonym 1	Antonym 2

Note 5 Words from **Puzzle 25**

Words	Antonym 1	Antonym 2

Challenge #3

Wonderful, this monster challenge is nothing to you!

Ready for the last one? Choose your 10 favorite words discovered in any of the Puzzles and note them below.

1.	6.
2.	7.
3.	8.
4.	9.
5.	10.

Now, using these words and within a maximum of six sentences, your challenge is to compose a text about a person, animal or place that you love!

Tip: You can use the last blank page of this book as a draft!

Your Writing:

Explore a Unique Store
Set Up **FOR YOU!**

MEGA DEALS

BestActivityBooks.com/**TheStore**

Designed for Entertainment!

Light Up Your Brain With Unique **Gift Ideas**.

Access **Surprising** And **Essential Supplies!**

CHECK OUT OUR MONTHLY SELECTION NOW!

- Expertly Crafted Products -

NOTEBOOK:

SEE YOU SOON!

Linguas Classics Team

BESTACTIVITYBOOKS.COM/FREEGAMES